Key Stage 3

Early Modern Britain

1509–1760

Robert Peal

William Collins' dream of knowledge for all began with the publication of his first book in 1819. A self-educated mill worker, he not only enriched millions of lives, but also founded a flourishing publishing house. Today, staying true to this spirit, Collins books are packed with inspiration, innovation and practical expertise. They place you at the centre of a world of possibility and give you exactly what you need to explore it.

Collins. Freedom to teach

Published by Collins
An imprint of HarperCollins*Publishers*
The News Building
1 London Bridge Street
London SE1 9GF

10 9 8 7 6 5

ISBN 978-0-00-819524-3

A catalogue record for this book is available from the British Library

Publisher: Katie Sergeant
Editor: Hannah Dove
Author: Robert Peal
Fact-checker: Barbara Hibbert
Copy-editor: Sally Clifford
Image researcher: Alison Prior
Proof-reader: Ros and Chris Davies
Cover designer: Angela English
Cover image: © Victoria and Albert Museum, London
Production controller: Rachel Weaver
Typesetter: QBS
Printed and bound by CPI Group (UK) Ltd, Croydon, CR0 4YY

Contents

Introduction

'Printing, gunpowder and the compass: These three have changed the whole face and state of things throughout the world; the first in literature, the second in warfare, the third in navigation; whence have followed innumerable changes...'

Francis Bacon, *Novum Organum*, 1620

Student Book 2 of Knowing History sees Britain enter a period of dizzying change. It begins with the coronation of Henry VIII in 1509, when England was a small Catholic country, ruled by the Tudors, and cautiously emerging from the medieval period. It ends in 1760, when England was part of a newly created Protestant country called Great Britain, ruled by the Georgians, and on the cusp of becoming a global empire.

Along the way, you will learn how Parliament, having nearly been blown up by Guy Fawkes, entered into a civil war against King Charles I – ending 8 years later with the execution of the king. You will learn how during the decades that followed, Parliament overtook the monarchy to become the most powerful institution in England. And you will learn how European sailors first reached East Asia by sea, and crossed the Atlantic to find a whole continent that had previously been unknown to them – America.

During this period of dramatic religious, political, and geographical change, you will have front row seats in the slow unveiling of the modern world. You will accompany great explorers such as Marco Polo and Cristopher Columbus on their voyages; follow the dilemmas and decisions of monarchs such as Henry VIII and Elizabeth I; and witness acts of great cruelty, such as the treatment of the native populations of the Americas, or the burning at the stake of Protestants for their religious beliefs.

The world today is as it is because of what has happened in the past. In studying history you may even start to see events in the present mirroring events in the past. As it is often said, history does not repeat itself, but it does sometimes rhyme.

Robert Peal, author of Knowing History

Concise chapter introductions set the scene and focus your learning.

Engaging photos illustrate the key ideas.

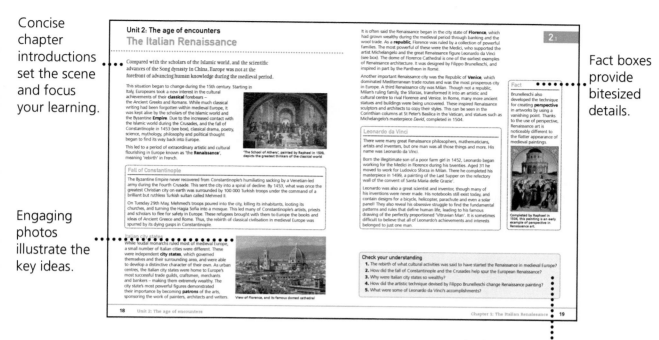

Fact boxes provide bitesized details.

End-of-chapter questions are designed to check and consolidate your understanding.

Timelines map out the key dates from the unit, and help you understand the course of events.

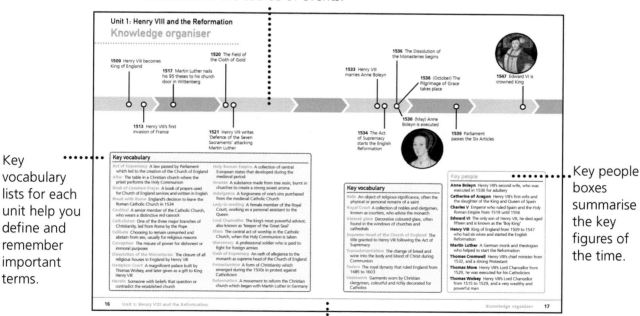

Key vocabulary lists for each unit help you define and remember important terms.

Key people boxes summarise the key figures of the time.

Knowledge organisers can be used to revise and quiz yourself on key dates, definitions and descriptions.

Unit 1: Henry VIII and the Reformation
The young Henry VIII

When Henry VIII was crowned king in 1509, he was already the hero of **Tudor** England. He was tall and handsome, and a keen jouster, wrestler, archer, hunter and tennis player.

Henry VIII was taught by some of the greatest philosophers of the age, and could write poetry, compose music and speak French and Latin fluently. The scholar Thomas More wrote a poem to celebrate Henry's coronation, stating: "This day is the end of our slavery, the fount of liberty; the end of sadness, the beginning of joy". High hopes rested on the young king's shoulders.

Henry was not meant to be king, but he became heir to the throne aged 10 when his older brother Arthur died unexpectedly in 1502. When his father Henry VII died, Henry VIII inherited the throne. Straight away, Henry married his dead brother's widow, Catherine of Aragon. Catherine was a pretty and intelligent Spanish princess six years his senior, and their marriage secured England's alliance with Spain.

Henry was 17-years-old when he became king. He ruled over a magnificent court, with continual entertainments and parties. Henry ordered regular jousting tournaments, which he often took part in himself. All of this jousting had a serious purpose, however: Henry VIII was training his noblemen for war. The new king dreamed of conquest, transforming England into a great European empire, ruling over Wales, Scotland, Ireland and France.

Portrait of Henry VIII, painted shortly after his coronation

War with France

Having allied with Spain and the **Holy Roman Empire**, Henry invaded France in 1513. The English army captured two towns, and won a victory against the French at the Battle of the Spurs. Henry's allies had changed their minds, however, and decided not to invade France. This left the English army unable to advance any further. Henry signed a peace treaty with France, securing new lands and an annual payment for England.

During the invasion of France, the Scottish King James IV (who was allied with France) took the opportunity to invade northern England with a large army of 60 000 men. With Henry absent, Queen Catherine organised England's defence against the Scots. The Scottish army was soundly beaten at the Battle of Flodden with thousands killed, including the Scottish King James IV. Catherine organised for the Scottish king's bloodstained tunic to be sent as a gift to Henry VIII in France.

The Field of the Cloth of Gold

Victories over the French and Scottish in 1513 confirmed England's position as a major European power. Henry VIII's dream of empire was edging ever closer. But events took a bad turn in 1516 when France gained a new king, the warlike and shrewd Francis I. Henry's **Lord Chancellor**, Thomas Wolsey (see box), persuaded Henry to make peace with France.

> **Fact**
>
> In 2004, a historian looking through an inventory of Henry VIII's royal wardrobe made a surprising find: the king, who loved sport, owned a pair of leather football boots.

Henry was reluctant to let go of his ambitions. To make the peace between England and France seem more honourable, Wolsey organised a magnificent celebration of peace. In June 1520, Henry VIII and Francis I met in France. For two weeks the young kings tried to outdo each other with displays of wealth and flamboyance. Henry and Francis even met each other in the wrestling ring, where Francis I won, much to Henry's anger. Many of the tents in which the visitors stayed were made from cloth threaded with gold, so the event became known as the 'Field of the Cloth of Gold'.

'The Field of the Cloth of Gold', painted for Henry VIII in 1545

Thomas Wolsey

Masterminding Henry VIII's early successes was a priest named Thomas Wolsey. The son of an Ipswich butcher, Wolsey rose from humble beginnings to become the most powerful man in England, aside from the king.

In 1514 Wolsey became Archbishop of York. The following year, the Pope made him a **Cardinal** and Henry appointed him Lord Chancellor, the king's chief advisor. Through sheer drive, Wolsey had gained complete control of English politics and the church. He worked tirelessly, organising the affairs of state so that Henry could enjoy himself. Whatever the king wanted, Wolsey would deliver.

Wolsey became magnificently rich, and liked to show off his wealth, travelling through London each morning in a grand procession flanked by two silver crosses. He built himself a house beside the River Thames, which was grander and larger than any belonging to the king. Wolsey named it **Hampton Court** Palace. Many in Henry's court were envious of Wolsey, resenting the fact that this 'butcher's boy' had risen to such wealth and power. His enemies nicknamed him the 'fat maggot', and began to plot his downfall.

Check your understanding

1. Who was Henry VIII's first wife, Catherine of Aragon, previously married to?
2. What military successes did England enjoy in 1513?
3. Why did Cardinal Wolsey persuade Henry VIII to make peace with France?
4. What was the purpose of the Field of the Cloth of Gold celebrations in 1520?
5. What positions of power did Thomas Wolsey hold?

The Reformation

At the start of the 16th century, the Roman Catholic Church was the single most powerful organisation in Western Europe.

From the forests of Poland in the East, to the coast of Portugal in the West, this one religion held sway over millions of lives. At the head of the Catholic Church was the Pope, who lived in Rome and controlled a large swathe of central Italy. Catholics believed that the Pope was God's representative on Earth, and he held enormous power. During the medieval period, popes called for crusades, started wars, and could make or break European royal families. However, by 1500, the Roman Catholic Church had developed a reputation for **corruption**.

Corruption

The papacy had been taken over by wealthy, power-hungry popes who paid little attention to religion. Perhaps the most infamous was Pope Alexander VI, who was from a powerful Spanish family known as the Borgias. He threw all-night parties, stole money from the church, and had as many as ten children with his mistresses – even though the Pope, as a Catholic clergyman, was supposed to remain **celibate**.

Pope Alexander VI

In order to raise money, the Catholic Church sold **indulgences**. An indulgence was a certificate personally signed by the Pope, which a Christian could buy to gain forgiveness for their sins. You could even buy indulgences for dead relatives, to shorten their time in purgatory.

There was also a lively market for 'holy **relics**'. Normally said to be body parts of saints or Jesus Christ, these relics were rarely genuine. Churches would buy and sell the fingernail of Jesus Christ, part of the tree from the Garden of Eden, or a vial of the Virgin Mary's breast milk. Pilgrims would pay churches considerable amounts of money to see and touch these relics, believing they had divine powers.

Lastly, the Catholic Church was enormously wealthy. Even holy orders of nuns and monks, who were supposed to live a life of simplicity and poverty in monasteries and abbeys, could be found living in luxury. The Catholic clergy wore **vestments** made of finest silk and velvet, and Catholic churches were richly decorated, with gold **altars**, wall paintings, burning **incense** and **stained glass** windows.

Money was raised to build St Peter's Basilica in the Vatican from the sale of indulgences.

Protestantism

Some priests began to argue that the Catholic Church had strayed from the true word of Jesus Christ, and been turned rotten by wealth. Jesus Christ lived a life of simplicity and preached against greed, they argued, so should the Catholic Church not follow his example?

These priests attacked the Pope and the Catholic Church, giving sermons and writing short books explaining their beliefs. They were greatly aided by the newly invented printing press (see page 20), which allowed their books to spread throughout Europe. Due to their 'protest' against the authority of the Catholic Church, they were given the name 'Protestants'.

Protestantism was particularly powerful in Germany, Switzerland, Holland and Belgium, where priests such as John Calvin and Martin Luther (see box) gained large followings. They proposed a simpler form of Christianity, replacing ritual and superstition with the word of the Bible, and richly decorated church interiors with plain, whitewashed walls.

Fundamental to Protestantism was the belief that all Christians should have their own relationship with God, formed through regular reading of the Bible. However, within Roman **Catholicism** the Bible could only be read in Greek, Hebrew or Latin, and all services were conducted in Latin. So, in secret, Protestants began translating the Bible into their own languages. This movement to reform Christianity spread across Europe and became known as 'the **Reformation**'.

> ## Fact
>
> Counting up all of the relics from a particular saint, one Protestant tract concluded that the saint must have had six arms, and 26 fingers.

Martin Luther

Born in Germany, Martin Luther became a monk at the age of 22. In 1510 he visited Rome, and was appalled by the wealth and corruption that he saw there.

In 1517 Luther wrote a list of arguments, known as the '95 theses', attacking church abuses, in particular the selling of indulgences. Luther nailed the 95 theses to the door of his church in Wittenberg, and this event is often said to have marked the start of the Reformation. In 1522, at a meeting known as the Diet of Worms, Pope Leo X declared Luther a **heretic** and an outlaw. On leaving the court, Luther was ambushed and kidnapped. However, his kidnapper was a German prince who offered Luther a hiding place at Wartburg Castle. In 1525, Luther married a former nun named Katharina von Bora who had abandoned her convent. Together they had six children. Luther also began to translate the Bible into German. He finished his German Bible in 1534, by which time much of Germany had converted to Protestantism.

Modern illustration of Martin Luther and his 95 theses

Check your understanding

1. Why was Pope Alexander VI so infamous?
2. What was corrupt about the selling of indulgences?
3. How were Protestant churches different from Catholic churches?
4. Why did Protestants want to translate the Bible into their own languages?
5. What did Martin Luther do in 1517, which is said to have marked the start of the Reformation?

Unit 1: Henry VIII and the Reformation
Henry's 'Great Matter'

In 1522 Henry VIII invaded France again, only to be embarrassed when his ally, the Holy Roman Emperor Charles V, failed to turn up.

Catherine of Aragon

When Henry tried to raise money for a second invasion in 1525, there were riots across England, so the invasion had to be called off. Henry's hopes of conquering France were abandoned, and he was left humiliated and frustrated.

Henry's frustration off the battlefield was even more serious. His wife, Catherine of Aragon, was now 40 years old and had given him only one child who survived infancy – his daughter Mary. Henry desperately needed a male heir to continue the Tudor royal line, but by 1525 Catherine was unlikely to provide one.

By now, Henry had fallen in love with a younger, prettier woman called Anne Boleyn, who was a **lady-in-waiting** to Queen Catherine. Anne was highly educated, ambitious and flirtatious, teasing Henry that she would only make love to him if he took her as his wife. As part of the **royal court**, she was able to enrapture the king with her intelligence and wit. Before long, Henry was desperate to have Anne as his wife.

The 'Great Matter'

In order to marry Anne, Henry first had to divorce Catherine. But this had to be approved by Pope Clement. Unfortunately for Henry, Catherine of Aragon's nephew was the Holy Roman Emperor Charles V. He had recently captured Rome, taking Pope Clement as his prisoner. Charles ordered that on no account should Pope Clement allow Henry to divorce his aunt Catherine, and Clement obeyed.

Anne Boleyn

Henry was absolutely determined to gain a divorce, and called the issue his 'Great Matter'. He claimed that he had solid, religious grounds to do so. The book of Leviticus in the Bible states if a man marries his brother's widow, the couple will remain childless. Henry used this passage to argue

Modern illustration of Catherine of Aragon pleading her case against divorce

that his marriage to Catherine was never lawful in the first place, and God had cursed him by not providing a son. In 1527, Henry asked the Pope Clement to annul his marriage, but the Pope refused.

Wolsey's fall

Henry asked his Chancellor Thomas Wolsey to persuade the Pope to change his mind. However, even his supremely powerful Cardinal Wolsey failed to do so.

Henry was furious, and Wolsey rapidly fell from favour. To try to win back the king, Wolsey gave him his magnificent Hampton Court Palace as a gift, but it was not enough. Wolsey was stripped of his job as Lord Chancellor in 1529, and fled to York. In 1530 he was ordered to stand trial on a trumped up charge of treason. During his journey from York back to London, Wolsey died a broken man. With his last words, Wolsey said: "Had I but served my God with but half the zeal as I served my king, He would not in mine age have left me naked to mine enemies."

The Great Gatehouse at Hampton Court Palace

The break with Rome

For six long years, Henry tried and failed to get his divorce, but then he had a new idea. Anne Boleyn was a keen reader of Martin Luther's books. She, and many others, suggested to the king that if England were no longer a Catholic country, Henry would no longer need the Pope's approval to divorce.

Henry did not like Protestant ideas. In 1521, he wrote a book entitled 'Defence of the Seven Sacraments', which attacked Luther's ideas and defended the Pope. Henry had made it illegal to own Luther's books. He even burnt suspected Protestants at the stake for being heretics. Henry VIII's early defence of Catholicism earned him the title 'Defender of the Faith' from Pope Leo X.

However, as Henry was desperate for a divorce, and furious with the Pope, he began to see some benefits in Protestant ideas. He also realised that if the head of the English Church was not the Pope, it could be him.

In January 1533, Henry married Anne Boleyn in secret. The marriage was declared valid by the Archbishop of Canterbury, Thomas Cranmer, two months later. Then, in November 1534, Parliament passed the **Act of Supremacy**, one of the most important laws in English history. It confirmed England's **break with Rome**, and created a new Church of England. From now on England no longer belonged to the Roman Catholic Church, and Henry VIII was the **Supreme Head of the Church of England**.

> ### Fact
> Anne Boleyn had such a strong hold over the king's affection that many myths grew up around her. Some said she had six fingers and that she was a witch.

Check your understanding

1. Why was Henry VIII so dissatisfied with his marriage to Catherine of Aragon by 1525?
2. What prevented Henry VIII from being able to divorce Catherine of Aragon, and marry Anne Boleyn?
3. On what grounds did Henry VIII claim that his first marriage was not lawful?
4. Why did leaving the Roman Catholic Church provide a solution to Henry VIII's 'Great Matter'?
5. What did the 1534 Act of Supremacy confirm?

The English Reformation

To ensure full support for the Act of Supremacy, Henry VIII ordered that all public figures and clergymen swear the **Oath of Supremacy.**

This oath stated that Henry was the Supreme Head of the Church of England. Those who refused to swear were tried for treason and executed.

A group of Carthusian monks who were loyal to the Pope were among those who refused. As punishment, they were dragged through the streets of London, then hanged, drawn and quartered at Tyburn. The abbot's arm was brought back to the abbey, and nailed to the door. The monk's heads were placed on the spikes above London Bridge.

The most famous figure to refuse was Henry's great friend Sir Thomas More, who was one of the most celebrated writers and thinkers in England. More became Lord Chancellor after the downfall of Thomas Wolsey, but only lasted three years before stepping down in 1532. As a devout Roman Catholic, More could not accept Henry's marriage to Anne. In 1534 he refused to swear the Oath of Supremacy, and was locked in a dark, damp prison cell for 17 months. Henry pleaded with More to swear the Oath, but his conscience would not allow him to change his mind. More was tried for treason and executed in 1535. On the scaffold, More said: "I die the king's good servant, but God's servant first".

Thomas More, Lord Chancellor to Henry VIII until 1532

The Dissolution of the Monasteries

With Thomas Wolsey dead, and Sir Thomas More executed, Henry needed a new chief minister. He chose Thomas Cromwell, who was born the son of a Putney blacksmith, but rose to become Chancellor of the Exchequer. Cromwell had led an exciting life, working as a **mercenary**, wool merchant, banker and lawyer along the way.

A keen reader of Luther, Cromwell pushed for further Protestant reforms to the church. In particular, he proposed that all of England's monasteries and abbeys should be closed down. Monasteries had a 1000 year history of providing education, prayer and charity to the people of England. But they were also accused of excessive wealth and corruption. Many of England's 800 monasteries were enormously wealthy, owning magnificent treasures and a quarter of the land in England. If they were closed, Cromwell told Henry, this land and property would revert to the crown. Henry was in urgent need of money to fight more wars, so the **dissolution of the monasteries** began in 1536.

The king's men descended on the monasteries, stripping lead from their roofs, gold, silver and jewels from their altars, and selling their land to local landowners.

Ruins of Whitby Abbey, in Yorkshire England

Monks and nuns were given a small pension, and turned out onto the streets. Henry made himself enormously rich, increasing the crown's income by around £150,000 a year (perhaps £80 million in today's money). England's monasteries, once so magnificent, were left to crumble – the haunting ruins of these ancient buildings can still be seen across England today.

The Pilgrimage of Grace

For many in England, the destruction of England's monasteries was a step too far. In autumn 1536, a group of angry Catholics gathered together in Yorkshire, led by a young nobleman named Robert Aske. He and his followers occupied York. They then invited the expelled nuns and monks to return to their monasteries and resume Catholic observance.

Aske's followers became known as the 'Pilgrimage of Grace', and their numbers swelled to around 35 000 men. Many were armed, and they planned to march on London.

Henry VIII sent an army north to meet Aske and his rebel army. He promised that if they went home, they would be forgiven. However, Henry was growing increasingly cruel. A year later, when a much smaller rebellion took place, he took the opportunity to round up and kill 200 of those involved in Aske's rebellion. In Cumberland, 70 villagers were hanged from trees in their villages in front of their families. Robert Aske was hanged in chains from York Castle, and left to die in agonising pain.

Banner carried during the Pilgrimage of Grace, showing the Holy Wounds of Jesus Christ

Tudor schools

Before their dissolution, monasteries provided a basic education for boys from the surrounding area. To replace this service, wealthy businessmen and landowners established new 'grammar schools'. Over 300 such schools were established during the 16th century, with a strong focus on teaching Latin grammar and promoting the new Protestant faith. Many were named after Henry VIII's son, King Edward VI, and his daughter Queen Elizabeth I.

The school day normally stretched from 7 a.m. to 5 p.m., and no girls were allowed to attend. The main subjects were Latin, religion, arithmetic and music. Boys would write with a quill pen, made from a trimmed feather. Misbehaving pupils would be beaten with a birch, or rapped over the knuckles with a wooden rod.

Check your understanding

1. What happened to those in England who refused to swear the Oath of Supremacy?
2. Who was Thomas Cromwell, and what were his religious views?
3. How did Henry VIII gain from the Dissolution of the Monasteries?
4. Why did Robert Aske begin the Pilgrimage of Grace?
5. Why did the Dissolution of the Monasteries lead to the creation of so many new schools in England?

Henry VIII and Edward VI

Henry VIII's marriage to Anne Boleyn did not last long. Her independent character, which had so delighted Henry when he first met her, infuriated him once she was his wife.

Henry longed for a son, but when Anne gave birth in September 1533, the child was a girl. She was named Elizabeth after Henry's mother. Henry was so disappointed not to have a male heir, however, he refused to attend his daughter Elizabeth's christening.

Anne miscarried her next three children, and Henry's dislike for her grew. After three years of marriage, Anne was charged with multiple cases of adultery and treason, though she was almost certainly innocent. In May 1536, Anne was executed, along with four of her accused lovers. One day later, Henry became engaged to his third wife, Jane Seymour. Henry adored Jane. She was mild-mannered and affectionate, and in 1537 she provided Henry with the son he had always desired. They named him Edward.

Jane died soon after Edward's birth, and Henry went on to have three more wives but no more children. In 1540, he married Anne of Cleves, but there was little attraction between them: Henry said she looked like 'a Flanders mare'. They divorced six months later. Later that year Henry married Catherine Howard, but she was accused of adultery and beheaded in 1541. Finally, in 1543 Henry married Catherine Parr, who acted as a stepmother to his three children, and outlived Henry.

Henry the tyrant

During a jousting tournament at Greenwich Palace in 1536, Henry was crushed beneath his horse and suffered severe injuries. Unable to exercise, he grew enormously fat and developed a 54 inch waist, arthritis and painful ulcers. By the end of his life Henry was too overweight to walk, and had to be wheeled around his palace in a specially made machine.

During this period, Henry turned against Protestant ideas, and put the English Reformation into reverse. In 1539, Parliament passed the Six Articles, reasserting Catholic doctrines such as celibate priests and **transubstantiation**. A year later, Henry beheaded his chief minister Thomas Cromwell for his Protestant sympathies, and for organising Henry's failed marriage to Anne of Cleves.

Henry was becoming increasingly tyrannical, and between 1532–1540 he executed 330 people: Protestants were burnt at the stake for being heretics; Catholics were hanged, drawn and quartered for being traitors; and the king's relatives were beheaded for being seen as rivals to the throne.

Jane Seymour

Anne of Cleves

Catherine Howard

Catherine Parr

Fact

In 1532 Henry VIII passed a law ruling that murderers who used poison should be boiled to death.

On 28 January 1547, Henry died aged 55. His funeral was a full Catholic service, complete with incense and Latin chanting. By the end of his long and eventful reign, Henry had invaded France three times, married six different wives, executed a Lord Chancellor and a chief minister, amassed 55 royal palaces, founded the Royal Navy, made himself King of Ireland, and established the Church of England.

Edward VI

Following his death, Henry's only surviving son Edward became king. Edward was just nine years old. Known as the 'boy king' and the 'godly imp', Edward VI was very intelligent, and a far stronger believer in the Reformation than his father. Whilst Henry VIII had started the English Reformation, the Church of England remained Catholic throughout his reign. It simply did not recognise the authority of the Pope in Rome.

Edward VI passed further Protestant reforms to the English Church: priests were allowed to marry; the Catholic **Mass** was abolished; and church services in English became compulsory. He also authorised the first prayer book in English, Thomas Cranmer's **Book of Common Prayer**.

However, Edward was an unhealthy and weak child. Aged only 15, sores appeared across his body and he began to cough up blood. In 1553 Edward died, unmarried and childless. Henry VIII's nightmare of an unstable throne with no certain heir had become a reality.

Portrait of Edward VI

The end of the old faith

Once on the throne, Edward VI was advised by his uncle the Duke of Somerset and his strongly Protestant Archbishop of Canterbury Thomas Cranmer.

Any remaining Catholic features were rooted out of English churches. Altars, hanging crucifixes, shrines, rood screens and statues were burned, while stained glass windows were smashed and wall paintings whitewashed. Catholic rituals and ceremonies, such as Corpus Christi processions and 'creeping to the cross', were banned. To most of England's poor, illiterate population, these colourful practices were fundamental to their belief, but from now on, they were deprived of the religion they knew and loved.

Rosaries, holy water, relics and icons were all banned from the Church of England. The old faith of medieval England had gone, and in its place was a new religion based not on ritual and superstition, but on the word of the Bible.

Modern image of a wooden rosary

Check your understanding
1. On what grounds was Anne Boleyn executed in 1536?
2. Was Henry VIII's marriage to Jane Seymour a success?
3. How did Henry VIII's accident in 1536 change his appearance?
4. Why did Henry VIII execute his chief minister Thomas Cromwell in 1540?
5. How were Edward VI's religious views different from those of his father?

Unit 1: Henry VIII and the Reformation
Knowledge organiser

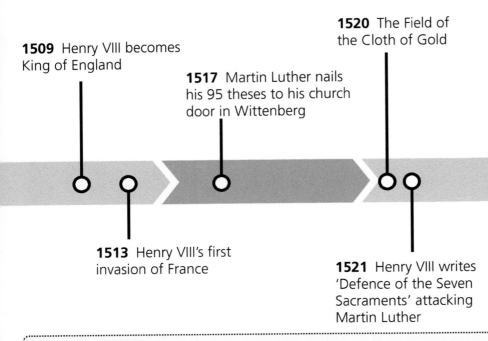

1509 Henry VIII becomes King of England

1513 Henry VIII's first invasion of France

1517 Martin Luther nails his 95 theses to his church door in Wittenberg

1520 The Field of the Cloth of Gold

1521 Henry VIII writes 'Defence of the Seven Sacraments' attacking Martin Luther

---

Key vocabulary

Act of Supremacy A law passed by Parliament which led to the creation of the Church of England

Altar The table in a Christian church where the priest performs the Holy Communion

Book of Common Prayer A book of prayers used for Church of England services and written in English

Break with Rome England's decision to leave the Roman Catholic Church in 1534

Cardinal A senior member of the Catholic Church, who wears a distinctive red cassock

Catholicism One of the three major branches of Christianity, led from Rome by the Pope

Celibate Choosing to remain unmarried and abstain from sex, usually for religious reasons

Corruption The misuse of power for dishonest or immoral purposes

Dissolution of the Monasteries The closure of all religious houses in England by Henry VIII

Hampton Court A magnificent palace built by Thomas Wolsey, and later given as a gift to King Henry VIII

Heretic Someone with beliefs that question or contradict the established church

Holy Roman Empire A collection of central European states that developed during the medieval period

Incense A substance made from tree resin, burnt in churches to create a strong sweet aroma

Indulgence A forgiveness of one's sins purchased from the medieval Catholic Church

Lady-in-waiting A female member of the Royal Court, working as a personal assistant to the Queen

Lord Chancellor The king's most powerful advisor, also known as 'keeper of the Great Seal'

Mass The central act of worship in the Catholic Church, when the Holy Communion is taken

Mercenary A professional soldier who is paid to fight for foreign armies

Oath of Supremacy An oath of allegiance to the monarch as supreme head of the Church of England

Protestantism A form of Christianity which emerged during the 1500s in protest against Catholicism

Reformation A movement to reform the Christian church which began with Martin Luther in Germany

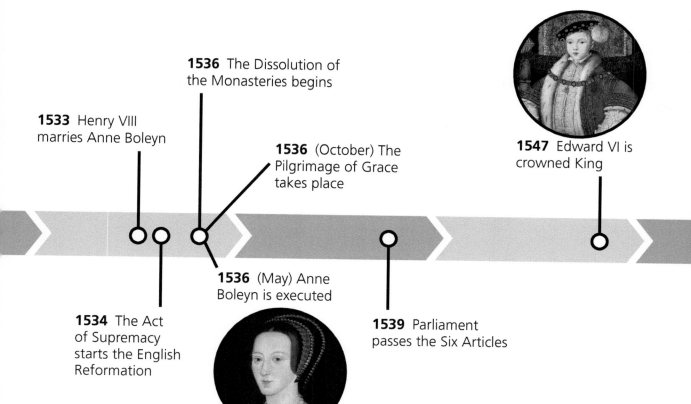

1536 The Dissolution of the Monasteries begins

1533 Henry VIII marries Anne Boleyn

1536 (October) The Pilgrimage of Grace takes place

1547 Edward VI is crowned King

1536 (May) Anne Boleyn is executed

1534 The Act of Supremacy starts the English Reformation

1539 Parliament passes the Six Articles

Key vocabulary

Relic An object of religious significance, often the physical or personal remains of a saint

Royal Court A collection of nobles and clergymen, known as courtiers, who advise the monarch

Stained glass Decorative coloured glass, often found in the windows of churches and cathedrals

Supreme Head of the Church of England The title granted to Henry VIII following the Act of Supremacy

Transubstantiation The change of bread and wine into the body and blood of Christ during Communion

Tudors The royal dynasty that ruled England from 1485 to 1603

Vestments Garments worn by Christian clergymen, colourful and richly decorated for Catholics

Key people

Anne Boleyn Henry VIII's second wife, who was executed in 1536 for adultery

Catherine of Aragon Henry VIII's first wife and the daughter of the King and Queen of Spain

Charles V Emperor who ruled Spain and the Holy Roman Empire from 1519 until 1556

Edward VI The only son of Henry VIII, he died aged fifteen and is known as the 'Boy King'

Henry VIII King of England from 1509 to 1547 who had six wives and started the English Reformation

Martin Luther A German monk and theologian who helped to start the Reformation

Thomas Cromwell Henry VIII's chief minister from 1532, and a strong Protestant

Thomas More Henry VIII's Lord Chancellor from 1529, he was executed for his Catholicism

Thomas Wolsey Henry VIII's Lord Chancellor from 1515 to 1529, and a very wealthy and powerful man

Unit 2: The age of encounters
The Italian Renaissance

Compared with the scholars of the Islamic world, and the scientific advances of the Song dynasty in China, Europe was not at the forefront of advancing human knowledge during the medieval period.

This situation began to change during the 15th century. Starting in Italy, Europeans took a new interest in the cultural achievements of their **classical** forebears – the Ancient Greeks and Romans. While much classical writing had been forgotten within medieval Europe, it was kept alive by the scholars of the Islamic world and the Byzantine **Empire**. Due to the increased contact with the Islamic world during the Crusades, and the fall of Constantinople in 1453 (see box), classical drama, poetry, science, mythology, philosophy and political thought began to find its way back into Europe.

This led to a period of extraordinary artistic and cultural flourishing in Europe known as 'the **Renaissance**', meaning 'rebirth' in French.

'The School of Athens', painted by Raphael in 1509, depicts the greatest thinkers of the classical world

Fall of Constantinople

The Byzantine Empire never recovered from Constantinople's humiliating sacking by a Venetian-led army during the Fourth Crusade. This sent the city into a spiral of decline. By 1453, what was once the greatest Christian city on earth was surrounded by 100 000 Turkish troops under the command of a brilliant but ruthless Turkish sultan called Mehmed II.

On Tuesday 29th May, Mehmed's troops poured into the city, killing its inhabitants, looting its churches, and turning the Hagia Sofia into a mosque. This led many of Constantinople's artists, priests and scholars to flee for safety in Europe. These refugees brought with them to Europe the books and ideas of Ancient Greece and Rome. Thus, the rebirth of classical civilisation in medieval Europe was spurred by its dying gasps in Constantinople.

Italian city states

While feudal monarchs ruled most of medieval Europe, a small number of Italian cities were different. These were independent **city states**, which governed themselves and their surrounding area, and were able to develop a distinctive character of their own. As urban centres, the Italian city states were home to Europe's most successful trade guilds, craftsmen, merchants and bankers – making them extremely wealthy. The city state's most powerful figures demonstrated their importance by becoming **patrons** of the arts, sponsoring the work of painters, architects and writers.

View of Florence, and its famous domed cathedral

It is often said the Renaissance began in the city state of **Florence**, which had grown wealthy during the medieval period through banking and the wool trade. As a **republic**, Florence was ruled by a collection of powerful families. The most powerful of these were the Medici, who supported the artist Michelangelo and the great Renaissance figure Leonardo da Vinci (see box). The dome of Florence Cathedral is one of the earliest examples of Renaissance architecture. It was designed by Filippo Brunelleschi, and inspired in part by the Pantheon in Rome.

Another important Renaissance city was the Republic of **Venice**, which dominated Mediterranean trade routes and was the most prosperous city in Europe. A third Renaissance city was Milan. Though not a republic, Milan's ruling family, the Sforzas, transformed it into an artistic and cultural centre to rival Florence and Venice. In Rome, many more ancient statues and buildings were being uncovered. These inspired Renaissance sculptors and architects to copy their styles. This can be seen in the Corinthian columns at St Peter's Basilica in the Vatican, and statues such as Michelangelo's masterpiece *David*, completed in 1504.

Leonardo da Vinci

There were many great Renaissance philosophers, mathematicians, artists and inventers, but one man was all those things and more. His name was Leonardo da Vinci.

Born the illegitimate son of a poor farm girl in 1452, Leonardo began working for the Medici in Florence during his twenties. Aged 31 he moved to work for Ludovico Sforza in Milan. There he completed his masterpiece in 1499, a painting of the Last Supper on the refectory wall of the convent of Santa Maria delle Grazie'.

Leonardo was also a great scientist and inventor, though many of his inventions were never made. His notebooks still exist today, and contain designs for a bicycle, helicopter, parachute and even a solar panel! They also reveal his obsessive struggle to find the fundamental patterns and rules that define human life, leading to his famous drawing of the perfectly proportioned 'Vitruvian Man'. It is sometimes difficult to believe that all of Leonardo's achievements and interests belonged to just one man.

Fact

Brunelleschi also developed the technique for creating **perspective** in artworks by using a vanishing point. Thanks to the use of perspective, Renaissance art is noticeably different to the flatter appearance of medieval paintings.

Completed by Raphael in 1504, this painting is an early example of perspective in Renaissance art.

Check your understanding

1. The rebirth of what cultural activities was said to have started the Renaissance in medieval Europe?
2. How did the fall of Constantinople and the Crusades help spur the European Renaissance?
3. Why were Italian city states so wealthy?
4. How did the artistic technique devised by Filippo Brunelleschi change Renaissance painting?
5. What were some of Leonardo da Vinci's accomplishments?

Unit 2: The age of encounters
Print, gunpowder and astronomy

Under the influence of the Renaissance, scholars increasingly broadened their concerns away from religious learning, and towards the study of mankind.

A new term emerged to describe this development: **humanism**. This change was helped by the growth of universities. The first European university was founded in the Italian city of Bologna in 1088, and universities in Oxford, Paris and Salamanca soon followed. By 1400, there were 53 universities in Europe, where students could study subjects such as law, philosophy, medicine and mathematics.

Printing Press

In medieval Europe, it took a monk up to three years to produce one handwritten Bible. For this reason, books were hugely expensive, and only the very wealthy or the very religious had access to them.

That was until Johannes Gutenberg, a metalworker from the German town of Mainz, started experimenting with printed text. The technology of printing with blocks of carved wood had arrived in Europe from China, but woodblock printing was time consuming and inefficient. Gutenberg's idea was to create equally sized individual letters out of metal that could be arranged and rearranged in a wooden frame to make whole pages of words, a technology known as '**movable-type printing**'. Gutenberg would then cover the metal type blocks with ink, and press onto them a sheet of paper, and then another, and then another.

Replica of an early printing press

In 1455, Gutenberg's **printing press** produced its first run of Bibles: 180 copies, each with 1286 pages. This started a **revolution**. By 1500, there were over 1000 printing presses in Western Europe, producing large numbers of books on religion, medicine, history, poetry, **astronomy**, and Latin grammar, sold at prices that many more than just the wealthy could afford. New ideas could now spread to many more people at an unprecedented speed. It is no coincidence that the Reformation began just half a century after Gutenberg's revolutionary invention.

Gunpowder

Gunpowder was invented in China, and first arrived in Europe during the 14th century.

During the siege of Constantinople in 1453, the Turkish Sultan Mehmed II employed a Hungarian engineer named Orban to build the largest cannon the world had ever seen. Measuring 29-foot-long and nicknamed 'The Imperial', it took a team of 60 oxen to haul Orban's cannon towards Constantinople. Once in position, 'The Imperial' fired stones weighing half a tonne towards the famous city walls of Constantinople. These walls had protected the Byzantines from invasion for a 1000 years, but after sustained cannon **bombardment**, they crumbled.

By the 16th century, gunpowder had conclusively spelled the end of medieval warfare. Faced with canon bombardment, even Europe's most feared castles were defenceless. Armed with a handgun, a lowly foot soldier could shoot dead a knight in shining armour. In 1620, the English scientist Francis Bacon wrote: "Printing, gunpowder and the compass: these three have changed the whole face and state of things throughout the world".

Astronomy

During the Renaissance, the ideas of the Greek astronomer Ptolemy were rediscovered. Ptolemy suggested that the heavenly bodies (sun, moon, planets, and stars) revolved around the earth, something known as a '**geocentric**' theory of space. The Roman Catholic Church welcomed Ptolemy's theory, as it placed God and the earth at the centre of the universe.

Surviving portion of the walls of Constantinople, in modern day Istanbul

However, a number of astronomers observed that the movement of the planets in the night sky was irregular, and they did not appear to orbit the earth. In 1543, Nicolaus Copernicus published a book called *The Revolution of the Heavenly Orbs*. In this book, Copernicus proposed a '**heliocentric**' theory, where the earth and the planets orbit the sun. The Catholic Church saw this as heresy, and banned Copernicus's book. But his troubling idea would not go away.

Galileo Galilei was a mathematics professor from Florence with an interest in astronomy. In 1609, he developed a new technology to observe the night sky: the telescope. Galileo openly supported Copernicus's heliocentric theory of the universe in his university lectures. In 1616 he was summoned to Rome where he was forced to deny his beliefs. Galileo was a committed Christian, so he agreed, but he could not sustain the lie. In 1632, he published *Dialogue concerning the Two Chief World Systems*. This book mocked the arguments of the Catholic Church, and explained Copernicus's heliocentric theory.

Galileo Galilei

Now a frail old man, Galileo was once again summoned to Rome. This time, he was threatened with torture, and after a series of interrogations, Galileo denied that the earth revolved around the sun. For his remaining years, Galileo lived under house arrest, and died in 1642.

> **Fact**
>
> The Catholic Church only formally ended their opposition to a heliocentric view of the universe in 1835.

Check your understanding

1. The growth of which institutions helped the spread of 'humanism' in medieval society?

2. Why did the invention of the printing press make books cheaper, and more efficient to produce?

3. Why did the invention of the printing press play an important role in the Reformation?

4. How did the use of gunpowder in Europe spell the end of medieval warfare?

5. What did astronomers observe, which made them propose a heliocentric theory of space?

Unit 2: The age of encounters
Global exploration

In medieval Europe, merchants could buy silk, spices and porcelain from faraway lands such as India and China. But merchants almost never visited these countries.

Goods from India and China were carried overland for thousands of miles along the '**Silk Road**'. This was not an actual road. Instead, it was a general route across central Asia, through the Islamic world, through Asia Minor to Constantinople, across the Mediterranean to Italy, and from there to the rest of Europe. The journey took years, during which time goods would have been bought and sold by merchants perhaps a dozen times, each time rising in price. By the time it arrived in Northern Europe, Chinese silk could be worn by only the wealthiest members of the nobility, and black pepper from India was an untold luxury.

Large parts of the Silk Road crossed through deserts, so camel trains were used to transport goods.

If a European merchant wanted to trade directly with India or China, they faced a perilous overland journey lasting years. For this reason, few ever attempted it.

Marco Polo

One exception to this was Marco Polo, the son of a Venetian jewel merchant. Aged just seventeen, Marco Polo set off with his father and uncle in 1271 on a mission to meet the Mongol Emperor Kublai Khan in his new capital city of Beijing. They were given a blessing from the Pope to convert Kublai Khan to Christianity.

Twenty-five years later, Marco Polo and his father returned to Venice. In 1298 Marco Polo published an account of his travels entitled *Description of the World*. The book captivated medieval Europe, and became a medieval bestseller. It told the extraordinary story of Marco Polo's journey to Beijing, his work as a military advisor to Kublai Khan, and his return to Europe escorting a Mongol princess to Persia. It also detailed the wealth of riches and luxuries to be found in China.

Venetian explorer Marco Polo

Ever since its publication, however, people have wondered how much truth there is to Marco Polo's fantastical adventures. Some parts are clearly made up, such as his account of Prester John, a mythical Christian king who never actually existed. As for the considerable time he spent in China, Polo accurately records their use of paper money and coal for fuel, but neglects to mention anything about chopsticks, Chinese characters for writing, or the Great Wall of China. In contemporary sources from all of the locations in China that Marco Polo claims to have visited, there is no single mention of a European advisor to Kublai Khan.

> **Fact**
>
> On his deathbed, Marco Polo's friends begged him to admit that his book was fiction, but he replied: 'I have not told half of what I saw.'

Sailing to India

True or not, it was clear from Marco Polo's stories that a great prize lay in wait for the first European merchant to establish a trading route with East Asia by sea. However, a large obstacle lay in the way: Africa. Navigation had slowly been improving during the medieval period, with the magnetic compass being used from the 13th century onwards. This, and the rediscovery of a description of world geography by the Greek astronomer Ptolemy, inspired an increased interest in sea exploration amongst Europeans.

The keenest medieval explorers were the Portuguese. Throughout the 15th century, Portuguese sailors travelled further and further down the west coast of Africa. None, however, was able to round the treacherous **Cape of Good Hope** at the tip of the African Continent, and sail on to India.

None, that was, until the Portuguese explorer Vasco da Gama, who was chosen to lead an expedition to India in 1497. On 8 July his fleet of four ships and 170 men left Lisbon. Almost one year later, he landed at Calicut in India, where they met the local king and exchanged European goods for a selection of Indian spices. After a horrendous journey home through the Indian monsoon, da Gama landed in Lisbon on 10 July 1499. Only 54 of his men had survived, but that did not matter to da Gama; he had become the first European to successfully sail to, and trade with, India.

In the years that followed, Portuguese sailors established a permanent trading post in Calicut, and terrorised the Muslim merchants who had previously dominated Indian Ocean trade. A new age of trade, **colonies** and empire was being born in Europe.

Portuguese explorer
Vasco da Gama

Sir John Mandeville

In 1371, a book was published containing the account of an English explorer called John Mandeville. He reported discovering a tribe who lived off the smell of apples, headless people with faces on their chests, and people with feet so large they used them as shade from the sun. The book was a bestseller, but Mandeville never existed, and his work was an elaborate hoax.

Check your understanding

1. Why were goods from China and India so expensive during the medieval period?
2. What story did Marco Polo's book *Description of the World* tell?
3. What obstacle prevented European merchants from sailing to East Asia?
4. Which country provided the keenest explorers in medieval Europe?
5. What historic feat did Vasco da Gama achieve in 1499?

Unit 2: The age of encounters
Christopher Columbus

Christopher Columbus was an Italian sailor from Genoa with one big idea: finding an alternative route to East Asia.

Contrary to popular myth, it was commonly understood in medieval Europe that the world was round. By this logic, Columbus believed the Indian Ocean could be reached by avoiding the Cape of Good Hope, and sailing due west across the Atlantic.

Known as the 'western passage', Columbus needed funding for his bold idea. He lived in Portugal, but the Portuguese King João II refused to back his voyage, as did the rulers of France, Venice, Genoa and England. Support finally came from King Ferdinand and Queen Isabella of Spain, who gave Columbus the money he required for a crew and three ships.

Statue of Christopher Columbus in Barcelona, Spain

Sea crossing

On 6 September 1492, Columbus set sail from the Canary Islands with 96 men, led by his flagship the *Santa Maria*. Imagine the terror and excitement they must have felt, setting sail across the vast expanse of the Atlantic Ocean and into the unknown.

Using the writings of Ptolemy as a guide, Columbus calculated that Japan lay just 2400 miles away, and would take four weeks to reach. In fact, Japan was 7000 miles away from Europe, and a whole unknown continent lay in between. Four weeks into the journey, Columbus and his men still had not seen land, and they were running out of fresh water. The crew were growing impatient, so Columbus agreed to continue sailing for four more days before turning home. Two days later, a sailor named Rodrigo de Triana sighted land.

Arrival in America

On 12 October, Columbus landed on the small Caribbean island of Guanahani. There, he found a peaceful **native** people called the **Taíno**, who did not wear clothes, and spent their lives farming, fishing, and smoking rolled up leaves of a then unknown plant called tobacco. Columbus sailed on to the nearby island of Hispaniola, where he found native people wearing small items of gold jewellery.

Columbus left 39 men on Hispaniola, and set sail back for Spain bringing with him evidence of his discovery to show Ferdinand and Isabella: gold jewellery, chilli peppers, sweet potatoes, parrots, and nine captured natives. Columbus's stories of a new land, and his hopes of finding greater reserves of gold, entranced the Spanish court. Having claimed that it was he, and not Rodrigo de Triana, who

Contemporary engraving of Christopher Columbus landing at Hispaniola in 1492

first sighted land, Columbus was rewarded with a pension of 10 000 silver pieces for every year until his death.

With the support of Pope Alexander VI, Ferdinand and Isabella claimed ownership of all lands discovered across the Atlantic. The Portuguese King João II insisted that Spain should share the spoils, so in 1494 the **Treaty of Tordesillas** was signed. This extraordinary agreement drew a line down the globe running 370 leagues west of the Cape Verde Islands. Anything west of the line belonged to Spain, anything east of the line belonged to Portugal. To this day, most of South America speaks Spanish, aside from an eastern bulge jutting out into the Atlantic called Brazil, which speaks Portuguese.

Columbus's legacy

In later life, Columbus became increasingly religious, and he took to dressing as a monk. Columbus refused to believe that the Bible could have failed to mention an entire continent, so he was never willing to accept that he had discovered a new land. Right up until his death in 1506, Columbus insisted that he had simply found the outer islands of East Asia. Columbus's mistake can still be heard in the language we use today: a string of Caribbean islands are known as the 'West Indies', and native Americans are commonly referred to as 'Indians'.

Modern illustration of Columbus's flagship the *Santa Maria*

Those explorers who followed Columbus would often describe the Americas as 'virgin' territory, meaning an untouched and uninhabited wilderness. This was only true because the native population had no immunity to diseases carried by the Europeans. The arrival of European settlers in the Americas caused an unintended genocide of catastrophic proportions.

Historians estimate that 90 percent of the native American population at the time of the European arrival died from new diseases such as measles, smallpox, malaria, and tuberculosis – perhaps 75 million in total. As for the Taíno, the Caribbean people who Columbus first encountered, within 18 years 99 percent of their population had perished. All that survives of them is a handful of words from their native language that are still in use today: canoe, hammock and barbecue.

Fact

Columbus was not the first European to reach America. Historians now agree that the Vikings got there nearly 500 years previously, but they never established permanent settlements.

Check your understanding

1. What route did Christopher Columbus believe he could take to sail to East Asia?
2. What did Columbus find when he landed on the island of Guanahani?
3. What was decided between Spain and Portugal by the Treaty of Tordesillas?
4. How is the error Columbus made when he discovered America reflected in words we use today?
5. Why did so many of the native people of the Americas die after Europeans made first contact?

Unit 2: The age of encounters
The 'New World'

Columbus's journey across the Atlantic blew the world wide open. Soon a constant stream of explorers was sailing from Portugal and Spain to explore these lands further.

In 1502, an Italian explorer, Amerigo Vespucci, who was working for the Portuguese sailed south along the coast of Brazil to the tip of **Patagonia**. Vespucci concluded that this was no outlying Asian island, but a whole new continent. When he returned to Lisbon in the spring of 1503, Vespucci wrote a letter to his friend, a member of the Medici family in Florence. Vespucci explained that Columbus was wrong, and that the land across the Atlantic was a '**New World**'.

The conquistadors

From 1516, Spain's ruler Charles V authorised further exploration of the American mainland, and his Spanish explorers became known as **conquistadors**.

In 1519, a conquistador named Hernán Cortes sailed from Cuba with 600 men, 16 horses and 14 cannon to explore the American mainland. Cortes arrived in Mexico, ruled at the time by the great **Aztec** Empire. Their capital was Tenochtitlán, a magnificent city of 200 000 inhabitants, built on an island in the middle of a lake. The Aztec emperor Montezuma had no reason to fear Cortes' piffling force, so he invited them into his city. Here, Cortes found enormous, unimaginable stockpiles of gold.

Relations between the Aztecs and the Spanish soured, and Montezuma was killed. Cortes fled the city, and returned in April 1521 with a much larger invasion force. Though the Aztecs were fearsome warriors, they were still a Stone Age civilisation. Cortes's army had steel swords, handguns and cannon, whilst the Aztecs had arrows, slings, and clubs made with sharpened volcanic stone. Cortes defeated the Aztecs, destroyed Tenochtitlán, and built a new, European style city in its place.

A similar story occurred when a Spanish conquistador called Francisco Pizarro landed in Peru, then ruled by another great civilisation, the **Inca** Empire. This time, European diseases had reached the native population before the Europeans themselves, and the Incas were ravaged by smallpox. In one of the most famously uneven battles in human history, Pizarro managed to defeat an Inca force of 80 000 with just 168 men, thanks to the panic and confusion caused by his cannon and galloping horses. The Incan emperor agreed to buy off the Spanish with rooms full of gold and silver.

Global trade

In the age of global exploration, Spain had won the lottery. Before long, a continual supply of gold and silver was flowing from their South American

> ### Fact
> Before long, the Latin version of Amerigo Vespucci's forename was being written onto maps to describe this New World: Americus, or America.

Ruined pyramids built by a native Mexican civilisation before the arrival of European settlers.

Ruins of Machu Picchu, a citadel built by the Incas on a mountain ridge, abandoned around the time of the Spanish Conquest.

colonies to the Spanish crown. As well as precious metals, the discovery of the New World brought new foods such as tomatoes, potatoes, chocolate, peanuts and vanilla, and new luxuries such as tobacco.

In countries where the local population was harder to subdue, the Spanish and Portuguese established coastal trading stations instead of colonies. Known as factories, these spread along the coasts of West and East Africa, India, China, Malaysia, Indonesia and the Philippines (named after Mary I's husband King Philip II of Spain). Portugal and Spain would dominate overseas trade for most of the 16th century, building the world's first truly global empires.

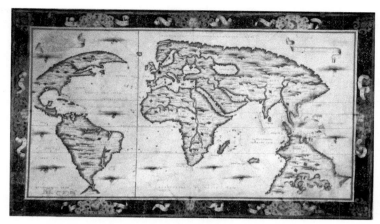

Map of the world, created in France in 1566

Ferdinand Magellan

In September 1519, a Portuguese sailor working for the Spanish set sail with five ships and 265 men for Indonesia, then known as the Spice Islands. Ferdinand Magellan plotted an audacious route heading west not east, intending to be the first European to sail around the tip of South America.

Magellan sailed towards Patagonia, where he claimed to encounter a race of giants, twice the size of Europeans. He then found a narrow channel leading to the other side of the continent. Freezing cold and beset with storms, the Magellan Strait, as it became known, is a dangerous route to sail. One ship sank, and another turned back. But after 38 days, Magellan and his men came out the other side, reaching an enormous ocean, which seemed calm in comparison. So they called it the Pacific, meaning 'peaceful'.

In March 1521, Magellan and his men reached the Philippines, where a local chieftain asked them to help him in a war against a rival tribe. Magellan agreed, but was killed by poisoned arrows during the battle. In September 1522, a single ship from Magellan's original expedition finally returned to Spain, with just 18 surviving men on board. However, they had earned their place in history as the first crew to **circumnavigate** the world.

Check your understanding

1. How did America gain its name?
2. How did the Pacific Ocean gain its name?
3. What advantages did Hernán Cortes and his conquistadors have when fighting the Aztecs?
4. Why were the Inca already weakened by the Europeans before Pizarro arrived in Peru?
5. What sort of goods, which are common in Europe today, originated in the New World?

Unit 2: The age of encounters
Knowledge organiser

1453 The fall of Constantinople

1455 The Gutenberg bible is printed in Mainz

1492 Christopher Columbus crosses the Atlantic and lands in America

1494 Spain and Portugal sign the Treaty of Tordesillas

1498 Leonardo da Vinci completes 'the Last Supper'

1499 Vasco da Gama returns from his voyage to India

Key vocabulary

Astronomy The science of studying extraterrestrial objects, and the universe

Aztec Native American civilisation who ruled much of what is today called Mexico

Bombardment To attack continuously a place with missiles until it gives way

Cape of Good Hope The southern tip of Africa, notorious for its stormy weather and rough seas

Circumnavigate To sail around something, often used to mean sailing around the world

City state A political system where a single city governs itself and its surrounding territories

Classical Relating to the art, culture or history of Ancient Greece and Rome

Colony A country or area under the political control of a foreign country

Conquistadors Spanish soldiers who led the conquest of the Americas

Empire A group of countries or states presided over by a single ruler

Florence Italian city state and banking centre where the Renaissance was said to have begun

Geocentric A system in astronomy where the earth is at the centre of the universe

Heliocentric A system in astronomy where the sun is at the centre of the universe, or solar system

Humanism A system of thought which concentrates on the human realm, often in place of religion

Inca Native American civilisation who ruled much of what is today called Peru

Movable-type printing A system of printing that uses and rearranges individual letters and punctuation

Native A person born in, or historically associated with, a particular country or region

New World Term given to North and South America following Columbus's voyage in 1492

Patagonia Region at the southern tip of the South American continent

Patron Someone who gives financial support to a person or institution, most often an artist

Perspective A method in art of depicting three-dimensional objects, often using a vanishing point

Printing Press A revolutionary invention, first created by Johannes Gutenberg around 1455

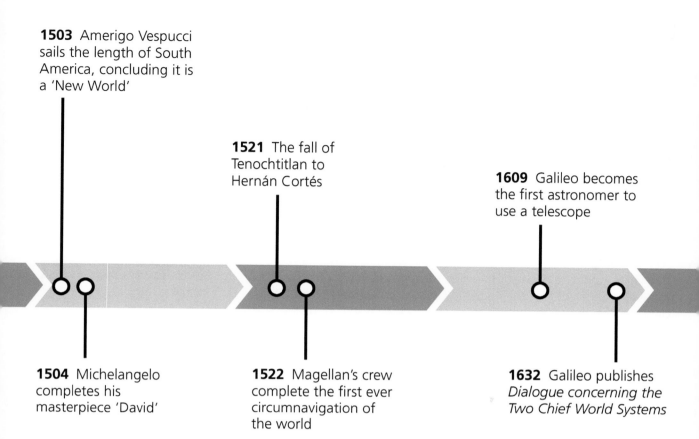

1503 Amerigo Vespucci sails the length of South America, concluding it is a 'New World'

1521 The fall of Tenochtitlan to Hernán Cortés

1609 Galileo becomes the first astronomer to use a telescope

1504 Michelangelo completes his masterpiece 'David'

1522 Magellan's crew complete the first ever circumnavigation of the world

1632 Galileo publishes *Dialogue concerning the Two Chief World Systems*

Key vocabulary

Renaissance Literally meaning 'rebirth', a period of cultural flourishing in late medieval Europe

Republic A state where the ruler is not a monarch, but comes from amongst the people

Revolution A change which means that nothing will ever be the same again

Silk road An ancient overground trade route which linked East Asia with the west

Taíno The native people of the Caribbean, wiped out by European diseases

Treaty of Tordesillas A treaty that divided the new world between Spain and Portugal

Venice City in northern Italy that dominated Mediterranean trade during the medieval period

Key people

Christopher Columbus Explorer who crossed the Atlantic and claimed the land he encountered for Spain

Filippo Brunelleschi Renaissance architect and artist who pioneered the use of perspective

Galileo Galilei Italian astronomer who supported a heliocentric theory of the universe

Hernán Cortes Spanish conquistador who defeated the Aztecs

Johannes Gutenberg German publisher who introduced movable-type printing to Europe

Leonardo da Vinci Renaissance genius who painted the Last Supper

Marco Polo Italian explorer who wrote a bestselling medieval book about his journey to China

Mehmed II Turkish sultan who conquered Constantinople

Vasco da Gama The first European to establish an overseas trading route with India

Mary I's Counter-reformation

During Edward VI's reign, his older sister Mary clung to her Roman Catholic faith.

She still attended Catholic mass in her private chapel even though it had been ruled illegal by her brother. When Edward told Mary off for this during a Christmas family dinner, she broke down in tears asking Edward to kill her before he forced her to give up her Catholic faith.

On his deathbed, Edward VI ruled that his Protestant cousin Lady Jane Grey should be his heir. However, the great majority of England's population thought that their rightful Queen was Edward's half-sister Mary, and an army of around 20 000 men gathered to support her. After just nine days, Lady Jane Grey gave up her claim to the throne, and Mary became queen in July 1553. Lady Jane Grey was locked in the Tower of London, forever to be remembered as the 'nine-days queen'.

Portrait of Mary I

Marriage and rebellion

After Henry VIII had divorced Mary's mother Catherine of Aragon, the 17-year-old Mary was ignored by her father and banned from seeing her mother. To make matters worse, Anne Boleyn soon gave Mary a prettier, cleverer, Protestant half-sister called Elizabeth. As Mary became more bitter and resentful, her attachment to Catholicism grew.

To prevent Elizabeth from succeeding her as Queen, Mary desperately needed to produce an heir. Mary intended to marry Philip II of Spain, the son of the Holy Roman Emperor Charles V. Philip was determined to defend the Catholic faith against the spread of Protestantism – a movement known as the **counter-reformation**.

A Catholic Spaniard was set to become king of England, and for many this was too much to bear. A knight called Sir Thomas Wyatt led a rebellion against Mary, but was defeated and captured in February 1554. Mary responded brutally: 120 rebels were hanged, and their bodies left to rot on the gallows in their home villages as a warning to others. Mary imprisoned her sister Elizabeth in the Tower of London, and executed her cousin Lady Jane Grey.

Portrait of Philip II of Spain

The Wyatt rebellion was a turning point in Mary's religious policy. In July 1554 she married Phillip, and confident that she would have an heir, Mary set about achieving a wholesale return of Catholicism to England.

'Bloody' Mary

Twenty years of religious reforms were put into reverse: churches were ordered to celebrate Mass and hold services in Latin; *The Book of Common Prayer* was outlawed; and priests who had married were forced to give up their wives. In November 1554, the heresy laws returned, and Protestants were once again burned at the stake.

English monarchs had used **burning at the stake** to punish heretics since the 1400s, but none used it quite as much as Mary. It was an agonisingly slow death, during which victims could feel, see and smell their flesh burn right before their eyes, suffering up to an hour of torturous pain before they died. Some witnesses reported seeing victims' blood boiling and steam bursting through the veins of their bodies.

In all, Mary had 283 Protestants burned at the stake, including 56 women, in five years. The most famous victim was Thomas Cranmer, the former Archbishop of Canterbury. Cranmer was England's leading Protestant and had masterminded Henry VIII's divorce from Mary's mother, Catherine of Aragon. This had made Mary's teenage years a misery. Even though Cranmer renounced his Protestant faith six times, Mary still had him burned.

Mary suffered a number of miscarriages, and failed to have a child. Her husband Philip abandoned her and returned to Spain. On 17 November 1558, Mary died. To her Catholic supporters, she was remembered as 'Mary the Pious', but to her Protestant opponents she would always be remembered as 'Bloody' Mary.

Illustration of William Sautre being burned at the stake for heresy

Foxe's Book of Martyrs

John Foxe was a Protestant cleric who fled to Switzerland during Mary's reign. He wrote a bestselling account of the period in 1563. It was a powerful work of Protestant **propaganda**, which helped to establish Mary's reputation as 'Bloody'.

The book tells in vivid detail how each Protestant **martyr** died. One account describes the burning at the stake of two bishops, Latimer and Ridley. Friends of the two bishops tied bags of gunpowder around their necks to ensure a quick death, but the wet wood burned too slowly. Latimer was heard calling out to his dying friend,

Execution of the Duke of Suffolk, from Foxe's book

'We shall this day light such a candle as I trust shall never be put out.'

Fact

In the last year of her life, Mary had a pain and a large lump in her stomach. She was convinced it was a child, but it was in fact the tumour that killed her.

Check your understanding

1. How were Mary I's religious views different from those of her half-brother Edward VI?
2. Why did the Wyatt rebellion take place in 1554?
3. Why did Mary I's religious policy become more pro-Catholic, and anti-Protestant, from July 1554 onwards?
4. Why was being 'burned at the stake' such an agonising death?
5. What religious viewpoint was Foxe's Book of Martyrs written to support?

Unit 3: The later Tudors
Elizabeth I

In 1558, the throne passed to Mary's steely and independent-minded half-sister, Elizabeth I. She made a series of thoughtful decisions that would ensure the stability of her 44-year reign.

Coronation portrait of Elizabeth I

The most pressing issue facing Elizabeth was England's religion. In her lifetime, England had moved away from Catholicism and then back again under her father, much further towards Protestantism under her brother, and then back to Catholicism under her sister. When Elizabeth came to the throne, England was split between those Protestants who wanted to see the Reformation taken further, and those who still had a deep affection for Catholic ceremonies and rituals.

Elizabeth's religious policy, known as the '**Elizabethan Religious Settlement**', was a masterstroke of compromise. Elizabeth established a Church of England that was Protestant in doctrine, but Catholic in appearance. Cranmer's Book of Common Prayer returned, services were conducted in English, Catholic ceremonies and rituals were banned, and priests were allowed to marry. However, bishops were retained, priests could wear traditional vestments, and church decorations such as stained glass windows were permitted.

At first, Catholics were not forced to convert to Protestantism. Attendance at Protestant services on Sunday was compulsory, but the punishment for not attending was kept low: a fine of 12 pence. Elizabeth was willing to turn a blind eye to Catholics who worshipped in private. As her advisor Sir Francis Bacon explained, she was not interested in creating 'windows into men's souls'.

Marriage

The next challenge was marriage. Elizabeth's Protestant advisors, such as her loyal Secretary of State William Cecil, were desperate for Elizabeth to marry and produce an heir. An endless supply of English noblemen and European princes wanted Elizabeth's hand in marriage, but none was quite right.

Marrying a European royal such as Philip II of Spain or Prince Eric XIV of Sweden would have made England overly attached to a foreign power. Marrying an Englishman such as Robert Dudley, the Earl of Leicester, would have caused jealousy and conflict at home.

Though none of her advisors agreed with her, Elizabeth believed that she could serve England best by providing a long period of stability but no heir. Elizabeth's stubborn determination won out. As she told her court favourite Robert Dudley: "I will have here but one mistress and no master".

Mary Queen of Scots

In 1570, the Pope issued a **Papal Bull** against the 'pretended Queen of England', declaring Elizabeth to be a heretic. It ordered English Catholics not to follow their queen, or risk being expelled from the Catholic Church.

Some English Catholics were driven to plot to kill the Queen, assured that this was the right path in the eyes of God. Elizabeth's government was thrown into panic. The greatest threat to Elizabeth was her Catholic younger cousin, Mary Queen of Scots (not to be confused with her half-sister Mary I). In 1568, Mary Queen of Scots was expelled from Scotland, and sought protection in England. Elizabeth was duty bound to offer shelter to her cousin, but Elizabeth also knew that some Catholics intended to kill her and place Mary Queen of Scots on the throne. So, for years Elizabeth imprisoned her cousin Mary in various **stately homes** and castles across England.

Portrait of Mary Queen of Scots

Elizabeth's government uncovered numerous Catholic plots to kill the queen, including one involving her own court doctor! After years of trying, Elizabeth's chief spymaster Francis Walsingham finally found the evidence he needed to implicate Mary. She had been communicating with a Catholic named Sir Anthony Babington who planned to assassinate Elizabeth I. They used coded letters, smuggled in and out of her prison in a waterproof case at the bottom of barrels, which Walsingham's spies managed to decode. In 1587, after 19 years of imprisonment, Mary Queen of Scots was beheaded.

As more and more plots against her life were uncovered, Elizabeth became increasingly intolerant towards Catholics. Fines for non-attendance at church increased, and in 1585 being a Catholic priest in England was made a crime punishable by death. In all, 180 Catholics were killed during Elizabeth's reign.

> **Fact**
>
> In many stately homes today, you can still see 'priest holes', where Catholic families would hide visiting priests, sometimes for days on end.

Francis Walsingham

Walsingham was Queen Elizabeth's chief 'spymaster', and had a network of spies across Europe. Walsingham would torture captured Catholics for further information. The Catholic priest Edmund Campion had iron spikes driven under his finger and toenails, and was placed on the **rack**. A Catholic from York named Margaret Clitherow was tortured by having a door put on top of her, and heavier and heavier weights were placed on the door until she died.

Check your understanding

1. What aspects of Catholicism did the Protestant Church of England retain under Elizabeth I?
2. Why did Elizabeth I believe neither a foreign nor an English husband would be suitable for her?
3. Why did the 1570 Papal Bull cause Elizabeth I's life to be in further danger?
4. What led to Mary Queen of Scots finally being sentenced to death in 1587?
5. How did Elizabeth I's treatment of Catholics in England change over the course of her reign?

Unit 3: The later Tudors
The Elizabethan Golden Age

Due to Elizabeth I's wise decision making, England enjoyed an unprecedented period of peace and stability during her reign.

Art, trade and culture all flourished in England, and this period is sometimes termed the 'Elizabethan **Golden Age**'. Religious plays had been a strong part of the Catholic Church, but they were banned during the English Reformation. As a result, secular theatre became increasingly popular. Wealthy nobles would hire troupes of travelling actors to provide them with entertainment.

The theatre

In 1576, London gained its first public theatre. Built in the London suburb of Shoreditch and called The Theatre, it lay safely outside the city of London, where theatre had been banned. Theatre was very different during the Elizabethan period, with drinks and food sold in the stalls, and plenty of interaction between the actors and the audience. Rowdy audiences would cheer, boo and pelt poor performers with food. Elizabeth I enjoyed the theatre, and the best performances in London's public theatres would be transferred to perform at the royal court.

One of the few surviving portraits of William Shakespeare

There were many famous playwrights of this period, but none more so than William Shakespeare. Between 1590 and 1613, he wrote 38 plays including comedies such as *Much Ado About Nothing* and *A Midsummer Night's Dream*, tragedies such as *Hamlet* and *Macbeth*, and histories such as *Henry V* and *Richard III*. Little is known about Shakespeare's life, but he is thought to have gone to a grammar school in Stratford-Upon-Avon, before going to London to work as an actor. Many phrases that we still use today originated with Shakespeare, such as 'vanished into thin air', 'tongue-tied' and 'the game is up'.

The Elizabethan court

The Queen's favourite noblemen and advisors together made up the royal court. They would stay together in the Queen's various palaces, and enjoy glittering entertainments, such as plays, dancing, jousting, hunting, banqueting and concerts. Elizabeth I liked to surround herself with brilliant and handsome young men, such as Sir Walter Raleigh.

Raleigh was a dashing soldier, who had fought for the Protestants in France (known as Huguenots) during the **Wars of Religion**. He was 6 foot tall, had dark curly hair, and wore a pearl earring in one ear. In 1578, he sailed to the Americas, and returned with a collection of presents for the Queen, including two Native Americans and some potatoes. Raleigh also returned with tobacco, and made smoking a fashionable pastime in Elizabeth's Court. Sir Walter Raleigh entranced Elizabeth with his charm, and many suspected Elizabeth was in love with him. When

Portrait of Sir Walter Raleigh

Elizabeth discovered that Raleigh had secretly married, she flew into a jealous rage and threw him in jail.

During the summer, Elizabeth would embark on her magnificent 'Royal **progresses**', being hosted by members of her royal court across England. Favourites who wanted to impress the Queen spared no expense entertaining her at their stately homes, such as William Cecil's Burghley House.

Gloriana

By 1601, Queen Elizabeth was growing old. She was called to Parliament that year, as many of its members were angry with the high taxes needed to pay for war with Ireland. Elizabeth quelled their anger by delivering what became known as her Golden Speech. It concluded: "And though you have had, and may have, many mightier and wiser princes sitting in this seat, yet you never had, nor shall have, any that will love you better."

Aware that it was probably the last time they would hear their queen speak, the Members of Parliament lined up to kiss Elizabeth's hand as they left, many in tears. Two years later, Elizabeth died. After decades of religious conflict, she brought peace to England. Today, Elizabeth is remembered as one of England's greatest rulers.

Illustration of Queen Elizabeth I in procession with her courtiers

Sir Francis Drake

Francis Drake was the greatest explorer of Elizabethan England. A tough young sailor from Devon, Drake worked for Queen Elizabeth as a '**privateer**', raiding Spanish **galleons** and trade ports in the Americas and returning to England with their cargo.

In an epic journey from 1577 to 1580, Drake became the first Englishman to circumnavigate the globe on his ship the ***Golden Hind***. Having sailed through the treacherous Magellan Strait, Drake captured an unprotected Spanish galleon full of gold off the coast of Peru. When he returned from his voyage, Drake moored the *Golden Hind* in Deptford, and invited the Queen to join him for dinner on board. Elizabeth knighted Francis Drake on board the deck of his own ship.

Fact

In one famous story, Sir Walter Raleigh saved Elizabeth I from walking through a muddy puddle by throwing down his cape so that she could walk over it.

Check your understanding

1. Why did the theatre become increasingly popular during Elizabeth I's reign?
2. How was the theatre different during the Tudor period compared with the theatre today?
3. What were Queen Elizabeth's 'progresses'?
4. In what ways were Sir Walter Raleigh and Sir Francis Drake similar?
5. What did Elizabeth I tell the Members of Parliament during her Golden Speech?

The Spanish Armada

During Elizabeth I's reign, Philip II of Spain was the most powerful king in Europe. He was a leading defender of Catholicism in the European Wars of Religion.

As a devout Catholic, Philip II had many reasons to dislike England. He had briefly been King of England until the death of Mary I. Philip courted Elizabeth I as his next wife, but Elizabeth rejected Philip's advances. Elizabeth gave English support to Protestant armies fighting in Europe, and she openly ordered English privateers such as Francis Drake to attack and rob Spanish ships of their precious cargo whilst returning from the Americas.

When Elizabeth executed Mary Queen of Scots in 1587, this seemed to guarantee a Protestant future for England. Philip II knew he would have to act fast if England was to return to the old faith.

The Armada

Philip set about building the largest naval invasion force Europe had ever seen. On 28 May 1588, it set sail from Lisbon for England. Named the 'Spanish **Armada**', Philip's force consisted of 130 large ships known as 'galleons', 8000 sailors and 18 000 soldiers. However, it had one crucial weakness: the commander of the fleet, the Duke of Medina Sidonia, had little sailing experience. He even suffered from sea-sickness.

In Holland, the Spanish had a crack-force of 30 000 experienced soldiers under the command of the Duke of Parma. Philip's plan was for the Armada to sail to France where he would meet the Duke of Parma's army, and then invade England. The English navy, under the command of Lord Howard of Effingham and Francis Drake, numbered 200 ships. Though more numerous, their ships were smaller, and had much less gun-power.

After weeks of waiting, the Spanish Armada was sighted off the coast of Cornwall on 19 July. A series of hilltop bonfires called 'signalling towers' were lit. This spread the news towards London and across the south coast: England was under attack.

That evening, the Spanish approached the English fleet moored in Portsmouth. With the wind blowing into the harbour, the English were vulnerable to attack, and the Spanish had their best chance of a quick and easy victory. However, Medina Sidonia wanted to stick to his orders to meet the Duke of Parma in France first, so he sailed straight past the English fleet.

Painting of English and Spanish ships during the Armada, completed shortly after the event

For a week, the English chased the Spanish up the channel, engaging in a few skirmishes. Then, on the 27 July, the Spanish anchored off Calais to pick up their reinforcements. To their shock, the Duke of Parma had not yet arrived. His army of 30 000 men was nowhere to be seen.

English victory

The following evening, on the 28 July, the English devised a tactical masterstroke. They filled eight ships with gunpowder and tar, creating '**hellburners**'. In the middle of the night, these were set on a course for the Spanish ships anchored at Calais. The Spanish commanders awoke to see the burning ships speeding towards them, and panicked. They cut their anchors and were scattered along the channel.

Modern illustration of the English hellburners

As a consequence, the Spanish lost their powerful 'crescent' formation, and were easy to attack. On the 7 August, the two sides met at the Battle of Gravelines, where the smaller English ships sailed rings around the larger Spanish galleons, sinking five and damaging many more.

At this point, Medina Sidonia made a serious navigational error, and the Armada was blown north towards Scotland. They then had to sail past Scotland and down the west coast of Ireland to safety, but were caught in treacherous storms. Around 60 Spanish ships were wrecked on the Scottish and Irish coasts, and 11 000 Spanish soldiers died. It is sometimes claimed that people living on the west coast of Ireland today are descended from Spanish sailors who were shipwrecked during the Armada.

Tilbury speech

The day after the Battle of Gravelines, Elizabeth I visited her troops who were stationed at Tilbury and awaiting the invasion. Dressed in a silver suit of armour, Elizabeth delivered the most famous speech of her reign. In it she declared: *"I know I have the body of a weak and feeble woman; but I have the heart and stomach of a king – and of a King of England too."*

Little did Elizabeth know, the English Royal Navy had already defeated the Spanish Armada. Had they not, Philip II may well have deposed Elizabeth I, and returned England to Catholicism. The history of England could have been very different indeed.

Fact

A year before the Armada, Francis Drake made a first strike on the Spanish fleet harboured in the Spanish port of Cadiz. Drake took them by surprise, sank 30 ships and set fire to the city. He boasted that he had 'singed the King of Spain's beard'.

Check your understanding

1. Why did Philip II of Spain want to invade England?

2. Why was it such a mistake for Medina Sidonia not to attack on the evening of 19th July?

3. Why did the English send 'hellburners' sailing towards the Spanish ships moored in Calais?

4. What happened to the Spanish Armada following the Battle of Gravelines?

5. What message did Elizabeth I deliver to the troops in her Tilbury Speech?

Rich and poor in Tudor England

By the time the Tudors came to power, some of England's most powerful noble families had died out during the Wars of the Roses.

Fewer noblemen meant fewer challenges to the monarchy, and the Tudor monarchs made sure that the nobility remained small and easily managed for the rest of their reigns.

When the Catholic Duke of Norfolk was executed in 1572 for treason, there were no more dukes left in England. By 1600, there was one marquess, 18 earls, two viscounts and 37 barons, making up a class of just 58 noblemen in the whole country. Most significantly, starting with the reign of Henry VII, it was illegal for noblemen to keep private armies. Many swapped their now unnecessary castles for stately homes. Tudor noblemen were still great landowners, but their days as an elite military class were over.

The gentry

The real ruling class of Tudor England was the **gentry**. Numbering around 15 000 families, members of the gentry were landowners without noble titles. Like the nobility, they made enough money from renting their land to tenant farmers to pursue lives of leisure. The gentry had the time to read and socialise, and called themselves 'gentlemen'.

Painting of a fair in Bermondsey, near London, from 1569

The decreasing power of the nobility during the Tudor period made it surprisingly easy for bright men of humble birth to rise to the top of society, as can be seen in the careers of Thomas Wolsey and Thomas Cromwell. Called '**new men**', many of these upwardly mobile Tudors benefited from the Dissolution of the Monasteries. It allowed them to buy church land cheaply and become landowning gentlemen.

The division between the landed wealthy and the working poor were as clear as ever in Tudor England. The medieval Sumptuary Laws remained in place, so only a nobleman could wear gold or silver cloth, and only a lord could wear red or blue velvet. At the other end of the scale, the Wool Cap Act of 1571 stated that all working people over the age of seven had to wear a wool cap on Sundays or holy days.

Painting of the diplomat Sir Henry Unton, with a rather large ruff

For the wealthy, fashions in Tudor England were always changing. During the reign of Henry VIII, men wore bulging sleeves and shoulder pads to make their upper body look powerful, along with enlarged codpieces to emphasise their masculinity. Men's fashion became more refined during the reign of Elizabeth I. Men began to wear short padded trousers called

hose, and a buttoned up jacket known as a **doublet**. From the 1560s onwards, any self-respecting lady or **gentleman** had to wear a **ruff**: an elaborate lace collar encircling the neck, which – as the playwright Ben Johnson observed – created the impression of a head on a plate.

Life for the poor

The population of England grew rapidly during this period, almost doubling from 2.4 million in 1520 to 4.1 million in 1600. This meant there were often not enough jobs to go round, so mass unemployment was common. To make matters worse, England's monasteries – which for centuries had cared for the poor during times of hardship – no longer existed.

Tudor woodcut showing a vagrant being whipped through the streets

As a result, travelling beggars called **vagrants** became a common sight in Tudor towns, and people in Tudor England often spoke of an increase in crime. At first, Tudor governments responded harshly. Begging was made illegal for everyone except the disabled or elderly. Able-bodied vagrants caught begging would have a large hole burnt through their right ear with a hot iron. If they reoffended, vagrants could be imprisoned or even executed.

The government did gradually begin to take more responsibility for the poor. From 1563 onwards, the '**Poor Laws**' were passed, requiring parishes to collect taxes from the local population, to provide help for the poor. The Tudors made a clear distinction between two different types of poor. The **'deserving' poor**, who were unable to work through old age, disability or the lack of jobs, were believed to deserve help. Whereas it was believed the 'undeserving' poor were simply idle, and deserved nothing.

Tudor football

Sport was very popular in Tudor England, in particular football. Aside from being played with a leather ball, there were few similarities with the modern game. Tudor football was often played between villages, with no boundaries to the pitch, and no limit to the number of players on each side. Players could pick up and run with the ball. Fights, broken bones, and even deaths were common.

Fact

Elizabeth I was no exception to the Tudor love of fashion. An inventory of the royal wardrobe in 1600 recorded that she owned 269 gowns, 96 cloaks, and 99 robes.

Check your understanding

1. Why was the nobility weaker during the Tudor period, than in the medieval period?
2. Why were landowners such as the nobility and gentry able to pursue lives of leisure?
3. How did men's fashions change from the reign of Henry VIII, to the reign of Elizabeth I?
4. Why was vagrancy such a problem during the 16th century?
5. What was the difference, according to the Poor Laws, between the deserving and the undeserving poor?

Unit 3: The later Tudors
Knowledge organiser

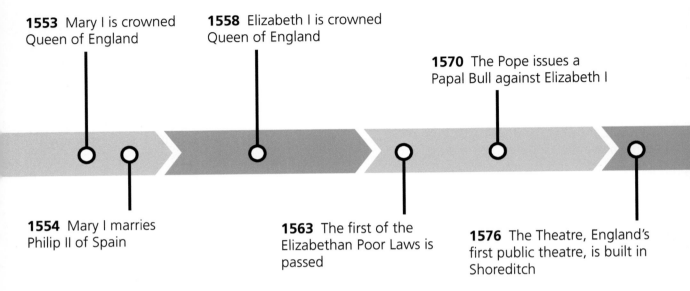

1553 Mary I is crowned Queen of England

1558 Elizabeth I is crowned Queen of England

1570 The Pope issues a Papal Bull against Elizabeth I

1554 Mary I marries Philip II of Spain

1563 The first of the Elizabethan Poor Laws is passed

1576 The Theatre, England's first public theatre, is built in Shoreditch

Key vocabulary

Armada Fleet of warships, often used to describe Spanish force sent to invade England in 1588

Babington Plot A foiled plot to kill Elizabeth I, which resulted in Mary Queen of Scots' execution

Burning at the stake A slow and painful execution, usually reserved for religious heretics

Counter-reformation Catholic fight back against the spread of Protestantism in Europe

Deserving poor Category developed by the Tudors for those amongst the poor in genuine need of help

Doublet and hose A buttoned up jacket and short padded trousers worn during the Tudor period

Elizabethan Religious Settlement A compromise agreement returning England to Protestantism but allowing Catholics to worship in secret

Foxe's Book of Martyrs A work of Protestant propaganda against Mary I, published in 1563

Galleon A large sailing ship, particularly from Spain

Gentleman Someone who earns enough money from land and investments not to work for a living

Gentry Class of wealthy landowners without noble titles, positioned just below the nobility

Gloriana A name given to Elizabeth towards the end of her reign, from the Latin for 'glorious'

Golden Age A period of flourishing in the history of a nation or an art form

Golden Hind Sir Francis Drake's ship, on which he completed his circumnavigation of the world

Hellburner A ship filled with explosives, set alight, abandoned and sailed towards the enemy

Martyr A person who is killed for their beliefs, often religious

New men Upwardly mobile men of the Tudor period, who benefitted from the weakening nobility

Papal Bull A formal and important announcement, issued by the Pope

Poor Laws Laws passed during the Tudor period, making local parishes raise money to help the poor

Privateer A private sailor or pirate, authorised by their government to attack enemy ships

Propaganda A piece of art or information used to promote a particular cause or point of view

Rack Torture device used slowly to stretch a person's body until all their joints dislocate

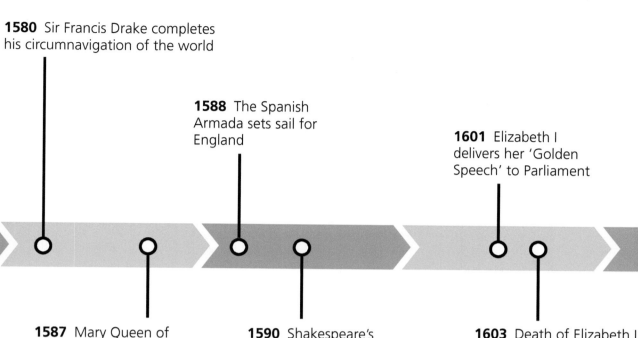

1580 Sir Francis Drake completes his circumnavigation of the world

1588 The Spanish Armada sets sail for England

1601 Elizabeth I delivers her 'Golden Speech' to Parliament

1587 Mary Queen of Scots is executed

1590 Shakespeare's first play, *Henry VI: Part I*, is performed

1603 Death of Elizabeth I

Key vocabulary

Royal Progress A summer journey taken by a monarch, visiting the stately homes of court favourites

Ruff An elaborate lace collar encircling the neck, fashionable during the Elizabethan period

Stately home A large country house at the centre of a gentleman or a noble's estate

Vagrant A person with no job, who travels from place to place begging

Wars of Religion A series of European wars fought between Protestants and Catholics from 1524 to 1648

Key people

Duke of Medina Sidonia Commander of the Spanish Armada, who suffered from seasickness

Elizabeth I Queen from 1558 to 1603, and remembered as one of England's greatest monarchs

Francis Walsingham Principal Secretary and 'spymaster' to Elizabeth I

Lady Jane Grey Cousin of Edward VI, known as the 'nine day Queen' for her very brief reign

Mary I Queen who led England's counter-reformation, and earned the epithet 'Bloody'

Mary Queen of Scots Elizabeth I's Catholic cousin and the most significant threat to her reign

Philip II of Spain King of Spain, who for a time was the husband of Mary I and King of England

Francis Drake Sailor and privateer, and the first Englishman to circumnavigate the globe

Walter Raleigh English sailor and explorer, and a noted favourite of Queen Elizabeth I

William Shakespeare Celebrated English playwright who worked during the Tudor and Stuart periods

James I and the Gunpowder Plot

Queen Elizabeth I died in 1603 leaving no direct heir to the throne. Her successor was to be found in Scotland, where the Protestant James VI was king.

James VI was the great-great-grandson of the first Tudor king, Henry VII, and the son of Mary Queen of Scots. In 1603, the 36-year-old King of Scotland became James I of England. His coronation in London united England and Scotland under the same monarch, but they were still two separate countries, with two separate **Parliaments**. James did not keep the Tudor name, but instead he used the name of his Scottish royal family: Stuart. The **Stuarts** would rule England for one hundred turbulent, war-torn years.

James's religion

People did not know what religious policy James I would pursue. His mother Mary was a Catholic martyr, but Mary had been imprisoned when James was just one-year-old. James was then brought up as a strict Protestant by his tutors. When James I came to the throne, English Catholics hoped that their new king would pursue a policy of **religious toleration** for Catholics. James's advisors, in particular his strongly Protestant Secretary of State Robert Cecil, made sure this was not the case.

Elizabeth I's anti-Catholic laws stayed in place: Catholic priests could be executed; dying Catholics could not be offered last rites; Catholics could not go to university; and Catholics who avoided Protestant church on Sundays would be fined £20 – an enormous sum of money at the time. By 1605, some English Catholics were desperate. They believed that only extreme action could ever return England to the old faith.

> ### Fact
>
> A significant landmark of James's reign was his authorisation of the King James Bible, which translated both the Old and the New Testament into English. Completed in 1611, it remains the most widely published book in the English language to this day.

The Gunpowder Plot

If it had been successful, the Gunpowder Plot would have been the most destructive terrorist attack in English history. Robert Catesby masterminded the plot, assembling a group of 12 Catholic plotters. The group included a battle-hardened soldier from York called Guy Fawkes. For 10 years Fawkes had fought as a mercenary for the Spanish Catholics against Dutch Protestants in the Wars of Religion, so was given responsibility for the explosives.

Contemporary engraving of the gunpowder plotters

Another plotter rented a cellar beneath the Houses of Parliament from a government official. Guy Fawkes packed the cellar with 36 barrels of gunpowder. The plan was to light the fuse on the morning of 5 November 1605. This was the same day as the **state opening of Parliament**, and the royal family, the royal court, and both houses of Parliament would all have been present. The explosion would have killed off most of England's ruling class, after which the plotters planned to put James I's daughter Princess Elizabeth on the throne as a puppet queen.

The letter

However, one of the plotters, named Francis Tresham, was worried that his brother-in-law Lord Monteagle would be at the state opening of Parliament. Tresham sent Lord Monteagle an anonymous letter telling him to think up an excuse not to attend Parliament that day, hinting that those who did attend "shall receive a terrible blow this Parliament and yet they shall not see who hurts them". On receiving the letter on 26 October, Lord Monteagle was suspicious, and immediately took it to Robert Cecil. Cecil waited until the morning of 5 November to act, when he sent the king's troops to search the cellars below Parliament.

FAC-SIMILE OF THE LETTER WRITTEN TO LORD MONTEAGLE
WHICH LED TO THE DISCOVERY OF THE GUNPOWDER PLOT.

Copy of the letter sent from Tresham to his brother-in-law Lord Monteagle

Here, Guy Fawkes was caught red-handed preparing to light the gunpowder fuse. Fawkes was seized, and tortured on the rack. After four days of agonising pain he confessed to his crime, and gave away the names of his fellow plotters. They were quickly tracked down by the king's men to a stately home in Staffordshire. Some were shot and killed whilst resisting arrest, and the surviving plotters were brought back to London where they were tried for **treason**. The plotters were hanged, drawn and quartered, with their hearts and intestines removed and burnt in front of them. Their heads were placed on spikes by London Bridge.

After such a close brush with death, any policy of toleration for Catholics in England was unthinkable for Parliament and the king. Anti-Catholic laws were strengthened. When Members of Parliament finally met, they instituted a 'public thanksgiving to almighty God every year on the fifth day of November'. This annual event took the form of bonfires, on which effigies of Guy Fawkes were burnt, giving birth to the English tradition of Bonfire Night.

Modern illustration of Guy Fawkes in the cellar below Parliament

Check your understanding

1. Why were England and Scotland ruled by the same king following the death of Elizabeth I?
2. Why were English Catholics particularly frustrated by James I's religious policy?
3. Why did the Gunpowder Plotters choose 5 November as the date to blow up Parliament?
4. How did Robert Cecil come to find out about the Gunpowder Plot?
5. What were the consequences, in terms of religious policy, of the Gunpowder Plot?

Unit 4: The English Civil War
Charles I and Parliament

Since at least the days of Magna Carta, most English monarchs had accepted that they should share power with the people they ruled.

Coming from Scotland, however, the Stuart kings thought differently. The Stuarts believed that because God was all-powerful, their family must have been chosen to rule England directly by God. To question them, therefore was to question God. This belief was called the **'Divine Right of Kings'**. King of Scotland, James I wrote a book called *The True Law of Free Monarchies*, which explained: "Kings are called Gods; they are appointed by God and answerable only to God".

Engraving of Charles I illustrating the Divine Right of Kings

Charles I

James I's son Charles was a shy and sickly child, who only learned to walk and talk at the age of four, and suffered from a stammer that would stay with him his entire life. He was crowned Charles I after the death of his father in 1625, and showed a fatal combination of bad judgement and stubbornness.

The early years of Charles I's reign were a catalogue of errors. In order to make peace with France, he married the daughter of the King of France, a Catholic named Henrietta Maria. War with France continued anyway, and many of England's Protestant population were now furious their king was married to a foreign Catholic.

Some even suspected Charles was a secret Catholic, who planned for the old faith to creep back into the Church of England. These suspicions increased when he appointed William Laud as Archbishop of Canterbury in 1633. Laud brought many aspects of Catholic services back into the Church of England, and sent inspectors to parishes across the country who would fine any priests not following his reforms. This disturbed the overwhelmingly Protestant people of England: it has been estimated that by this time 97 percent of England's population were Protestant, as were 88 percent of the nobility and gentry.

Most concerned by Charles's sympathy for Catholicism were England's **Puritans** (see box). Many Puritans sat in Parliament, where they repeatedly questioned Charles I's policies and tried to limit his power. By 1629, Charles was sick of Parliament questioning his divine right to rule. So, from 1629 until 1640 Charles ruled without calling Parliament once, a period known as the **'eleven-years tyranny'**. Charles wanted to be like the **absolutist** monarchs of Europe, such as the powerful Catholic Kings of France, Louis XIII and XIV.

> ### Fact
>
> To demonstrate their divine power, Stuart kings continued a medieval practice known as **'touching for the king's evil'**. This involved touching people with a skin disease called scrofula in order to heal them.

Charles I and his Catholic wife Henrietta Maria

Without Parliament, however, Charles had no means of raising new taxes. He found a clever way around this problem. There was an old tax called **'ship money'**, which was used to tax towns by the coast and build up the navy when England was under threat of invasion (such as during the Spanish Armada). Charles did not need Parliament's permission to raise ship money so, even though England was at peace, he extended it to all parts of the country. Soon, ship money was making Charles £200 000 a year, and he spent the money on anything but ships: in particular his fine clothing, new palaces and enormous art collection.

In 1637 John Hampden, a wealthy landowner and **Member of Parliament (MP)**, was imprisoned for refusing to pay ship money, and became a hero for Parliament's cause. Those who criticised Charles I could be called before his own personal court, the **Star Chamber**. When a Puritan lawyer called William Prynne published a book in 1632 which implied the king's dances were immoral, he was put on trial before the Star Chamber. Prynne was imprisoned for life, and had his face branded and both his ears chopped off. Charles I, some believed, was becoming a tyrant.

Puritans

During the 1600s, a radical form of Protestantism became popular in England. Its followers tried to live lives that were as godly and 'pure' as possible, so became known as 'Puritans'.

Puritans wanted a world of strict Christianity, a 'heaven on earth' with no sin or wickedness. They wore simple black clothing, as they believed that jewellery, make up and colourful clothing were sinful. Activities such as gambling, drunkenness, dancing, music, theatre and sport were also frowned upon, and on Sundays no activity was allowed except for reading the Bible

Portrait of a Puritan family from the 1640s by the Dutch artist Frans Hals

and going to church. Puritans did not believe the English Reformation had done enough to change the Church of England, and had a fierce dislike of Catholicism.

Because they were hard working, and did not spend much money, many Puritans became successful merchants and farmers. As they grew wealthier, Puritans gained more political power.

Check your understanding

1. What was meant by 'the Divine Right of Kings'?
2. What was misjudged about Charles I's decision to marry Henrietta Maria?
3. Why was the period between 1629 and 1640 known as the 'eleven-years tyranny'?
4. Why was Charles I's decision to collect taxation through ship money so controversial?
5. Why were England's Puritans gaining power during the Stuart period?

Unit 4: The English Civil War
The outbreak of war

From 1637 onwards, a series of events sent England tumbling towards **civil war**. It began with troubles north of the border, in Scotland.

The Reformation had been particularly strong in Scotland, where a form of Protestantism known as **Presbyterianism** had taken hold. From 1560, committees of clergymen and laymen ran the Church of Scotland, with no royally appointed bishops. James I and Charles I did manage to reintroduce some bishops to Scotland, but they did not have the power of English bishops.

To increase Charles I's power over the Church of Scotland, Archbishop Laud devised a new prayer book for Scotland, with some aspects of Catholic services. When Laud's prayer book was first used at St Giles Cathedral, Edinburgh in 1637, the Scottish congregation rioted. They threw wooden stools at the clergy, and accused them of 'popery'. Soon, there was an open rebellion against Charles I throughout Scotland, known as the **Bishops' War**. In 1640, a Scottish army marched across the border and occupied England as far south as Yorkshire.

The Long Parliament

Charles I urgently needed to raise an army and end the Bishops' War. However, for an army, he needed to raise new taxes, and to raise new taxes he needed Parliament. Charles recalled Parliament in April 1640, but dissolved it three weeks later after it refused to raise the money he needed for the Bishops' War. In September, Charles called Parliament again. This Parliament would remain in session, on and off, for the next 20 years. It became known as the **'Long Parliament'**.

Contemporary engraving of the execution of the Earl of Strafford

Charles only expected Parliament to meet and approve new taxes. After 11 years of being ignored, however, Members of Parliament had a long list of demands for the king. They wanted to meet every three years; they wanted an end to ship money; and they did not want the king to have the power to dissolve Parliament without their permission. Some Puritan Members of the Long Parliament, such as the lawyer John Pym, went even further. They asked for Bishops to be removed from the Church of England; all of Henrietta Maria's Catholic friends to be expelled from court; and for the tutors of Charles I's son – the future King of England – to be chosen by them.

Parliament also wanted to punish some of Charles's closest advisors. Archbishop Laud was accused of treason, and imprisoned in the Tower of London. Another of the king's favourites, the Earl of Strafford, was accused of negotiating with an army in Ireland to invade England and suppress opposition to the king. Parliament sentenced Strafford to death for treason, and forced Charles I to sign his friend's death warrant.

Arguments raged for another year, but neither Parliament nor the king would give in. Urged on by his queen Henrietta Maria, Charles decided on 4 January 1642 to show his strength by arresting, in person, the five most troublesome Members of Parliament, including John Pym and John Hampden. It was a catastrophic error of judgement. Charles marched into Parliament, sat in the Speaker's Chair, and read out their names. However, the MPs had been tipped off in advance, and escaped down the River Thames. Charles looked round Parliament in despair, and observed, "I see all my birds have flown".

Victorian painting of the failed arrest of the five Members of Parliament

The failed arrest of the five members was a disaster for Charles. It made him seem both weak and tyrannical. Over the following days, the people of London became increasingly agitated, building barricades, collecting weapons, and attacking the houses of suspected Catholics.

War

Charles decided it was no longer safe for his family to stay in London. On 10 January 1642, he fled for York. Parliament was effectively left in charge of the country. In March, Parliament passed the **'Militia Ordinance'** stating that the army was under their control. War, it seemed, was inevitable.

Different parts of England started to declare for either the 'Royalist' or the 'Parliamentarian' side. On 22 August, Charles I raised the King's standard in Nottingham – showing his intention to fight Parliament. The English Civil War had begun.

Civil wars are uniquely horrific events. Towns and families are split apart, pitching fathers against sons, brothers against brothers, and friends against friends. One in four English men fought at some point during the English Civil War. Around 11 000 houses were burned or demolished, including historic stately houses such as Basing House and Corfe Castle. 150 towns saw serious damage, and an estimated 5 percent of England's population died due to war or disease – a higher proportion than died during the First World War.

Fact

In 1641, Charles I travelled to Scotland to make peace with the leaders of the Bishops' War. Whilst there, he played a round of a popular Scottish sport called golf.

Check your understanding

1. What caused the Bishops' War to start in Scotland?
2. Why did the Bishops' War force Charles I to recall Parliament?
3. What sort of demands did Members of Parliament make once Parliament had been recalled?
4. Why was his attempt to arrest the five Members of Parliament such a catastrophe for Charles I?
5. What event marked the beginning of the English Civil War?

Unit 4: The English Civil War
Fighting the English Civil War

Having fled the city in January 1642, Charles I's primary objective at the beginning of the English Civil War was to retake London.

There were three major battles. The first conflict was at the Battle of Edgehill, just outside Warwickshire, in October 1642. The outcome of the battle was indecisive. When Charles I's weary army attempted to take London, it was repelled by local citizen militias called **trainbands** at Turnham Green.

The next major battle was at Marston Moor near York in July 1644. The war had been going the **Royalists'** way for two years, but at the Battle of Marston Moor the **Parliamentarians** won their first major victory against Charles. Prince Rupert's cavalry was routed – as Oliver Cromwell said, "God made them as stubble to our swords". After Marston Moor, the Parliamentarians gained control of northern England.

A year later in July 1645 the Parliamentarians delivered a killer blow to the Royalists at the Battle of Naseby near Leicester. Almost the entire Royalist army was killed or captured, and Parliament's troops seized the king's baggage train. Here, they found £100 000 in jewels and treasure, and the king's private correspondence.

Painting of Prince Rupert, the archetypal cavalier

Published later that year, Charles's letters showed he had been negotiating with Irish and French armies to invade England and put him back on the throne. In return, Charles had promised to repeal anti-Catholic laws. The king's enemies used this as evidence that Charles was planning treason against his own people, and they began to refer to him as 'Charles Stuart, that man of Blood'. After Naseby, Parliament seized the Royalist headquarters at Oxford. Charles I was left defeated and disgraced.

Cavalier

The Royalists, who fought for the king, were mostly recruited from the nobility, some Catholics, and people from the countryside. The Royalist cavalrymen were often of noble birth, and liked to have long hair and expensive clothing. They went into battle wearing knee high boots with high heels, colourful decorated tunics, soft leather gloves, shirts with ruffled cuffs, and beaver hats with ostrich feather plumes.

Like the knights of medieval Europe, Royalist cavalrymen saw themselves as romantic figures. They were nicknamed **'Cavaliers'** after the Spanish word 'caballero', meaning horseman. The archetypal cavalier was Prince Rupert, a nephew of Charles I's who travelled from Germany to England aged only 23 to command the Royalist cavalry.

> ### Fact
> Prince Rupert would take with him to battle his pet dog, a poodle called Boye, who some Roundheads believed had magical powers. Boye was captured and killed at the Battle of Marston Moor.

Prince Rupert was a flamboyant character. On the battlefield, he was a brave and skilled commander, but could get carried away. At the Battle of Edgehill, he chased the retreating Parliamentarian forces too far and lost his chance to win a real victory. At the Battle of Marston Moor, he was still having a dinner party with his officers when the Parliamentarians attacked.

Roundhead

The Parliamentarian soldiers were nicknamed **'Roundheads'**, due to the shaved heads of some of Parliament's supporters. Parliamentarians were mostly recruited from minor gentry or people living in towns, many of whom were Puritans. They had a more disciplined approach to war than the Cavaliers. Whilst the Cavaliers spent the first winter of the war throwing expensive parties, the Parliamentarians trained their army.

In 1645, a Puritan cavalry general called Oliver Cromwell set about creating a full-time Parliamentarian army. Called the **'New Model Army'**, they were strictly disciplined and devoted to Parliament's cause. Drinking and swearing were forbidden, and deserting was punished with public floggings. They were a professional army, with red uniforms, simple practical clothing, and metal armour. Cromwell's cavalry forces were so formidable, they were nicknamed the 'Ironsides'.

Most importantly, the New Model Army believed they were fighting in a holy war. They would sing hymns marching into battle, and read from the Bible or listen to sermons that inspired them to fight. Promotion in the New Model Army was gained not through wealth or high-birth, but through merit. As Cromwell said:

Modern illustration of Parliamentarian soldiers

> "I would rather have a plain russet-coated captain that knows what he fights for, and loves what he knows, than that which you call a gentleman and is nothing else".

Political radicals

During the turmoil of the Civil War, some people developed political ideas that were surprisingly radical for the 17th century. One group argued for equal legal and political rights for all men. They were called the **'Levellers'**, as they wanted to level out the hierarchy of Stuart society. Another group, called the 'Diggers', established a religious community in Surrey with common ownership of all land and possessions.

Check your understanding

1. What was Charles I's main objective at the beginning of the English Civil War?

2. Why was Charles I left disgraced after the Battle of Naseby?

3. What was the character of Prince Rupert?

4. How did the approach of the Parliamentarian army differ from that of the Cavaliers?

5. How did the religious beliefs of the New Model Army influence their behaviour?

Trial and execution

After his defeat at the Battle of Naseby, Charles I surrendered to the Scots in April 1646. He believed the Scots would treat him better as a prisoner than Parliament would.

This marked the end of the first Civil War. In June, Parliament met with Charles I in Newcastle to discuss a peace settlement. Parliament put forward a set of demands, known as the **Newcastle Propositions** (see box), but Charles saw the demands as an insult. He refused them outright.

The Scots soon tired of holding Charles I as a prisoner, and sold him to Parliament for £400 000 in February 1647. The king was now Parliament's prisoner, but still they were unable to agree on a settlement. In November 1647, Charles I escaped from his prison in Hampton Court and rode south to the Isle of Wight. This sparked a second Civil War, and Royalist uprisings took place in Kent, Essex, Yorkshire, Wales and Cornwall. In addition, Charles I had secretly been negotiating with a Scottish army, who invaded England in support of the king. By September 1648, Parliament had won the second Civil War with a bloody three-day battle at Preston.

By now, the most extreme opponents to the king were not in Parliament, but in the army. The New Model Army had grown too large and powerful for Parliament to control, and when Parliament ordered the army to disband in 1646, it refused. Led by the Oliver Cromwell, the army began to argue that more radical action against Charles I was needed.

Rapier, a lightweight sword used during the English Civil war

> ## The Newcastle Propositions
>
> Some of the demands were:
>
> - The Church of England should no longer have bishops
> - Royalist estates be handed over to Parliament
> - Parliament should remain in control of the army for 20 years
> - Parliament should choose membership of the king's government

Trial

On 5 December, 1648, Parliament voted to continue negotiations with the king, but the army had other ideas. The following day a soldier called Colonel Pride invaded Parliament, arresting 45 Members of Parliament for supporting the king, and expelling a further 186 for supporting further negotiations.

'Pride's Purge', as it became known, was a crucial turning point. Now just 200 strong opponents of Charles II remained as Members of Parliament, and many were ready to try him for treason. When Cromwell was told that it was legally impossible to try a king, he replied "I tell you we will cut off his head with his crown upon it!".

The trial of Charles I began on 20 January, 1649, in Westminster Hall. Parliament was renamed the High Court of Justice, and Charles was tried for being "A tyrant, traitor, murderer and a public and implacable enemy to the commonwealth of England". The prosecution argued that Charles had begun the Civil War against his own people, and was therefore responsible for all of the death and destruction that followed. They also accused him of treason for conspiring with France and Ireland to invade England on his behalf.

Charles refused to answer the charges. He argued that because treason is defined as a crime against the king, it is impossible to try a king for treason. Even if Charles had defended himself, the verdict

Contemporary painting of the execution of Charles I by an unknown artist

was not in question after Pride's Purge. The remaining MPs appointed 135 commissioners to act as judges, but even then only 59 signed Charles I's death warrant. The others stayed away through fear or disapproval.

Execution

Charles was led to the executioner's block on 30 January 1649. The execution took place outside **Banqueting House**, a beautifully ornate part of the Palace of Whitehall built by Charles and his father James. The day was bitterly cold, and Charles asked to wear two shirts, so that he did not appear to be shivering with fear. Before his execution Charles declared, "I go from a corruptible to an incorruptible crown".

With one strike of the axe, his head was chopped off. There was a deathly silence, before soldiers began to disperse the spectators in order to avoid a riot. Many members of the crowd dipped their handkerchiefs in the king's blood, believing that it would have divine powers.

The crowd could not quite believe what they had seen. Due to the army's radicalisation, Charles I had been executed against the will of the great majority of England's population. It was as if England had become a republic by accident.

Fact

The chief judge at the trial of Charles I, John Bradshaw, was so worried about the threat to his life that he wore a beaver hat lined with steel and a suit of armour beneath his clothes.

Judge Bradshaw's steel-lined hat

Check your understanding

1. Why did Charles I refuse to agree to the Newcastle Propositions?
2. Why were Parliamentarians quickly losing patience with Charles I by September 1648?
3. On what grounds did Parliament try Charles I for treason in 1649?
4. Why did Charles I refuse to answer any of the charges during his trial?
5. What was the response of the London crowd to the execution of Charles I?

Unit 4: The English Civil War
Knowledge organiser

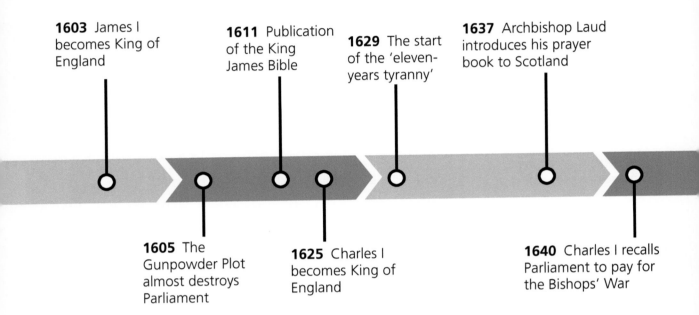

1603 James I becomes King of England

1611 Publication of the King James Bible

1629 The start of the 'eleven-years tyranny'

1637 Archbishop Laud introduces his prayer book to Scotland

1605 The Gunpowder Plot almost destroys Parliament

1625 Charles I becomes King of England

1640 Charles I recalls Parliament to pay for the Bishops' War

Key vocabulary

Absolutist A ruler who has absolute power over his or her people

Banqueting House Ornate building in the Palace of Whitehall outside which Charles I was executed

Bishops' War An uprising against Charles I's religious reforms which began in Scotland

Cavalier The nickname for Royalist cavalrymen during the English Civil War

Civil War A war between two sides from the same nation

Divine Right of Kings The theory that a monarch is appointed by God and should have absolute power

Levellers A radical group during the Civil War who demanded equal legal and political rights

Long Parliament A Parliament which met, on and off, from 1640–1660

Member of Parliament Someone elected to sit in the House of Commons, often abbreviated to 'MP'

Militia Ordinance A law by which the English Parliament took control of the army from Charles I

Newcastle Propositions A series of demands devised by Parliament in 1646, and rejected by Charles I

New Model Army A full-time, professional army formed by Oliver Cromwell during the Civil War

Parliament A collection of people representing all of England, who approve or refuse laws

Parliamentarians Those who are loyal to Parliament, often during a dispute with the king

Presbyterian A strong form of Protestantism that took root in Scotland following the Reformation

Pride's Purge The expulsion of all but the most radical Members of Parliament in December 1648

Puritan A group of radical Protestants who wore plain clothing and tried to live without sin

Religious toleration A policy of allowing many different religions to exist within one state or country

Roundhead The nickname for Parliamentarian soldiers during the English Civil War

Royalists Those who are loyal to the king, often during a dispute with Parliament

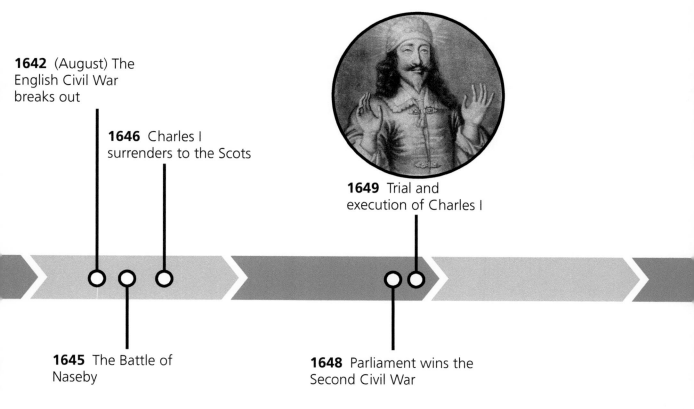

1642 (August) The English Civil War breaks out

1646 Charles I surrenders to the Scots

1649 Trial and execution of Charles I

1645 The Battle of Naseby

1648 Parliament wins the Second Civil War

Key vocabulary

Ship money A tax imposed on coastal towns to pay for their defence from naval attack

Star Chamber The English monarch's personal court, which did not have to give defendants a fair trial

State Opening of Parliament The ceremony where England's monarch opens a session of Parliament

Stuarts The royal dynasty ruling England from 1603 to 1714

The eleven-years tyranny A period from 1629 during which Charles I ruled without calling Parliament

Touching for the king's evil The healing touch of a king for those who suffer from skin disease

Trainbands The City of London's volunteer militia, who fought for Parliament during the Civil War

Treason A crime against your own people, nation, or monarch

Key people

Charles I The second Stuart King of England, executed by Parliament following the Civil War

Guy Fawkes A leading member of the Gunpowder Plot, given responsibility to guard the explosives

Henrietta Maria Queen to Charles I, she was a Catholic and from France

James I First Stuart King of England, and son of Mary Queen of Scots

John Hampden Member of Parliament, who was tried and imprisoned for not paying ship money

John Pym Puritan Member of Parliament, and major opponent to Charles I before the Civil War

Prince Rupert Charles I's German nephew, appointed commander of the Royalist cavalry aged only 23

William Laud Archbishop of Canterbury who reintroduced some Catholic practices into church services

Unit 5: Commonwealth and Restoration
Cromwell's Commonwealth

The execution of Charles I astonished the people of England who, for the first time in their history, were not ruled by a monarch.

Instead, England was ruled by 140 Members of Parliament, nicknamed the **'Rump Parliament'**, as only the most radical members had been allowed to remain following Pride's Purge. England was declared a **'Commonwealth'** on 16 May 1649, meaning it would be ruled in the common interest of the people. Three days later, the House of Lords was abolished. Many thought that they lived in a 'world turned upside-down'.

Ireland and Scotland

The Royalist cause still had strong support in Scotland and Ireland, and Parliament was afraid that England's neighbours could help Charles I's son (also named Charles) win back the crown. So, in 1649 they sent their best general, Oliver Cromwell, to defeat the Irish rebels.

Ireland was still a Catholic country. The only Protestants in Ireland were descended from Scottish and English settlers sent to Ireland by Elizabeth I and James I. These Protestant settlers had seized land from the native population, and mostly lived in the northern province of Ulster. Irish Catholics strongly disliked the Protestant settlers, and in 1641 there was an uprising against the Protestants known as the 'Portadown Massacre'.

Eight years later, Oliver Cromwell was out to seek revenge. Cromwell's treatment of the Irish Catholics was merciless. In the town of Drogheda, his troops killed 3500 civilians. Another 1500 civilians were killed in cold blood in Wexford. Worse still, Cromwell forced the Irish from their land, and those who resisted were sent to work as slaves on the Caribbean island of Barbados. Perhaps 200 000 Irish people died due to famine and war caused by Cromwell, and he is still remembered with hatred in many parts of Ireland today.

Cromwell saw things differently. He returned from his Irish campaign in 1650, and reported to Parliament "I am persuaded that this is a righteous judgement of God upon these barbarous wretches". A year later, Cromwell was sent to put down a rebellion in Scotland, where Royalists planned to invade England and put Charles I's son on the throne. Cromwell defeated the Scottish force twice, once at Dunbar in Scotland in 1650, and again at the Battle of Worcester in 1651. However, the young Charles managed to escape to France.

Lord Protector

Cromwell returned to England a war hero with 30 victories and no defeats on the battlefield. Cromwell believed in **'Godly Providence'**, meaning that everything on earth happened due to God's will. It was easy for Cromwell to believe that God wanted him to win battles.

Contemporary print of Oliver Cromwell, accusing him of assuming the powers of a king

He also believed that it was God's wish for him to rule England. So, in 1653 Cromwell dismissed Parliament and made himself **'Lord Protector'**. Many urged him to become King Oliver, but Cromwell could not bring himself to do so. As Lord Protector, Cromwell still wore his simple black clothing and grey woollen socks.

In 1655, Cromwell appointed 11 Major-Generals to rule over the different regions of Britain, and used them to impose his Puritan beliefs. He banned theatre, dancing and pubs. On Sunday, it became illegal to go to buy or sell goods, or take part in sports such as bowling, horseracing and football. Cromwell even banned Christmas celebrations, as he saw them as an excuse for drunkenness and gluttony. For the first and only time in English history, the country was under a **military dictatorship**.

Cromwell's death

In 1658 Oliver Cromwell, the simple farmer who rose to be king in all but name, died. His son Richard became Lord Protector, but Richard Cromwell was a weak ruler without the stern authority of his father. He was nicknamed 'Tumbledown Dick', and after less than a year, he stepped down under pressure from the army. Oliver Cromwell's attempt to turn England into a Commonwealth was coming to an end.

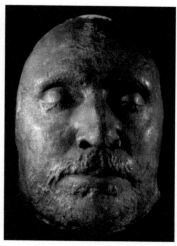

Death mask of Oliver Cromwell

Oliver Cromwell

Oliver Cromwell was a member of the minor gentry from Huntingdon, near Cambridge. As a young man he appears to have suffered from severe depression, and he only recovered after converting to Puritanism during the late 1620s. Cromwell became intensely religious, and was elected to Parliament in 1628. He was descended from the sister of Thomas Cromwell, Henry VIII's chief minister who dissolved the monasteries. Clearly, Protestantism ran in the Cromwell family's blood.

Cromwell was a straightforward man, and not very good looking. Famously, he had warts on his face and a big nose. When his portrait was being painted, Cromwell is believed to have told the painter to depict him 'warts and all'.

Fact

Cromwell did have a genuine belief in the freedom of worship. For this reason in 1655, Jews were allowed back into England for the first time since Edward I banished them in 1290.

Check your understanding

1. Why did Parliament send their army to Ireland and Scotland after the end of the English Civil War?
2. What were the religious beliefs of the people in Ireland during this period?
3. Why is Oliver Cromwell still remembered with hatred in Ireland today?
4. What did Cromwell do to Parliament in 1653?
5. Once he became Lord Protector, what did Cromwell do to impose his Puritan beliefs?

Unit 5: Commonwealth and Restoration
The Restoration

It was clear England's Commonwealth experiment had failed under the rule of Tumbledown Dick. So, in 1660 the first elections in almost 20 years were held, and Parliament began negotiations with Charles I's son.

Coronation portrait of Charles II

The younger Charles was living in **exile** in Holland. Straightaway, he showed more willingness to compromise than his father. He issued a series of promises for what he would do as king, known as the **Declaration of Breda**. Charles promised religious toleration; rule alongside Parliament; and, most importantly, to take no revenge on those Parliamentarians who fought during the Civil War. After 20 years of bloody conflict, Charles II's Declaration offered England a chance to wipe the slate clean, and Parliament was happy to agree.

On 29 May 1660, the king was welcomed into London by ecstatic crowds. The writer John Evelyn recorded in his diary, "With a triumph of above 20 000 horse and foot, brandishing their swords and shouting with inexpressible joy; the ways strewed with flowers, the bells ringing, the streets hung with tapestry, fountains running wine… I stood in the Strand and beheld it, and blessed God".

The English monarchy had been restored, so this period has become known as the **'Restoration'**. Once king, the only revenge Charles II took was to execute the 59 **regicides** who signed his father's death warrant.

The Merry Monarch

Charles II did not care much about religion, and had an enormous thirst for enjoying life. He was nicknamed the **'Merry Monarch'**. Charles II wore magnificent clothes with a wig of long curly black hair, and particularly enjoyed drinking, gambling, and dancing. He is known to have fathered at least 14 children with women who were not his wife. Once, when Charles II was introduced to an audience as 'Father of the English People', he joked that he had at least fathered a great number of them.

> **Fact**
>
> The regicides who had already died, including Oliver Cromwell, were exhumed, and had their corpses beheaded and their heads placed on spikes at Tyburn.

Charles was witty and charming. However, he was notoriously untrustworthy and lacked principles. As his friend, the drunken poet Lord Rochester wrote:

"We have a pretty witty king,
Whose word no man relies on;
He never said a foolish thing,
Nor ever did a wise one."

Painting of Charles II dancing with his sister Mary at a ball whilst in exile in Holland

As his reign continued, Charles II became less popular. His wild lifestyle and unsuccessful war against the Dutch caused high taxation. Charles II's financial situation became worse after London was hit by the plague in 1665, and the Great Fire in 1666. In 1667, England was humiliated when the Dutch navy sailed up the Medway and attacked the unsuspecting English navy, destroying half their ships and stealing the *Royal Charles* – England's greatest warship. However, nothing was quite so controversial as Charles II's approach to religion.

Religion

Charles II's French mother, Henrietta Maria, was a devout Catholic, and in 1668 his brother James, Duke of York secretly converted to Catholicism. In 1670, Charles II made a secret agreement with the French King Louis XIV promising to convert to Catholicism and to tolerate Catholics living in England. In return, Louis XIV paid Charles II 2 million *livres* every year.

Known as the **Treaty of Dover**, Charles kept his agreement a secret for many years, as there was a strong anti-Catholic feeling amongst the English people. After the English Civil War, enforcing conformity to the Church of England was seen as the only way of avoiding future conflict. In 1673, Parliament passed the **Test Act**, making allegiance to the Protestant Church of England compulsory for clergymen, teachers, and all those in government office. The king's own brother, James, Duke of York, had to step down as Lord High Admiral.

When Charles II died in 1685, he took the last rites of a Catholic. England was yet again faced with the same problem that dogged it for over a century. The dead monarch had no legitimate heir, and the next in line to the throne was a Catholic – his brother James.

Charles II's younger brother, James, Duke of York

Charles II's escape

The young Charles II was no stranger to adventure. After his defeat at the Battle of Worcester in 1651, he spent a night hiding in an oak tree. Disguised as a servant and calling himself Will Jackson, Charles travelled through England hunted by Parliament's troops and with a price of £1000 on his head. After six weeks he reached the coast, and sailed for France. Along the way ordinary people offered Charles II shelter, and this experience was said to have given him a rare ability to connect with his subjects.

Check your understanding

1. Why was Parliament happy to agree to Charles II returning to England as king in 1660?
2. How did Charles II deal with those who had fought for Parliament during the Civil War?
3. How would you describe the character of Charles II?
4. Why did Charles II keep his 1670 agreement with Louis XIV of France a secret?
5. Why was England faced with such a great problem after the death of Charles II in 1685?

Unit 5: Commonwealth and Restoration
Restoration England

After 10 years of Puritan rule, the English people welcomed the merry monarch Charles II. It was as if a grey cloud had been lifted from national life, allowing the sun to shine back in.

Alehouses, maypoles and Christmas celebrations all returned. Sunday sports were played, churches had music and choirs, local fairs were held, and theatres reopened. For the first time in English history, women were allowed to act on stage.

Fashions changed as well, as people once again wore colourful clothes, with lace, frills, silk and ribbons. Led by the king, a new fashion for wigs took off, and they became increasingly extravagant over the next 100 years. The Restoration is now remembered as a time of fun and frivolity.

Scientific revolution

In 1662, King Charles II gave a Royal Charter to a group of scientists, giving birth to the **Royal Society** of London for Improving Natural Knowledge. A great interest in science had developed in England during the 17th century. This was due in part to the Renaissance, but also to the Reformation, which encouraged people to move away from **superstition** and towards **rational thought**.

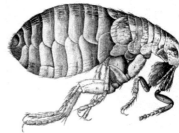

Robert Hooke's drawing of a flea, completed using his newly invented microscope in 1664

One member of the Royal Society was Robert Hooke, who built a compact microscope and was able to produce detailed drawings of insects, such as the flea. Earlier in the century, the English scientist William Harvey used a series of experiments to prove that blood circulates through the body, instead of being continually produced and consumed like fuel.

But the most important scientist of the period was, without doubt, Sir Isaac Newton. So the story goes, Newton was sitting under a tree when an apple fell on his head. This led him to wonder what forced the apple downwards, and the answer was gravity. Newton realised that all objects attract each other, depending on their mass and distance. This explains not only why an apple falls to the floor, but also why planets orbit the sun. Newton explained the laws of gravity, and much more, in a book entitled *Principia Mathematica* and published in 1687. It is often described as the most important book in the history of science.

Newton was the first English scientist to be knighted, but he remained very modest. He compared himself to a boy playing with pebbles on the seashore, aware that "the great ocean of truth lay all undiscovered before me".

Sir Isaac Newton

The Great Plague

In 1665, the plague returned to England, and spread like wildfire through London where human, animal and food waste was often left rotting in the narrow, crowded streets. Hygiene was non-existent, especially for the poor, and 68 000 people died in a single year. Those who could afford it fled the city, and King Charles II took his royal court to Oxford.

Just like the attack of the plague during the Black Death of 1348, people had no idea why they were dying. The most popular theory was that plague spread through bad air, known as **'miasma'**. Plague doctors visited patients in an outfit designed to protect them from miasma. It consisted of a heavy waxed overcoat, glass goggles, a wooden cane for touching victims, and a 'beak' stuffed with scented substances such as dried flowers – designed to mask the bad air.

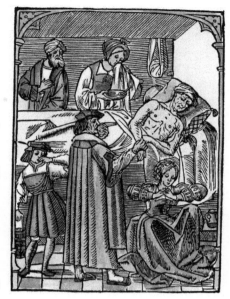

To prevent the spread of miasma, the mayor of London ordered that all dead bodies be collected and buried out of town, and the house in which they died be locked up and have a red cross painted on the door. Early each morning, body collectors roamed the streets of London ringing their bells and shouting, 'bring out your dead'. These measures had some positive effect in limiting the deaths, but it took a more destructive force to finally wipe out the plague: fire.

German print from the 16th century of a doctor treating a plague victim

Nell Gwyn

If one person summed up Restoration England, it was Charles II's mistress Nell Gwyn. An orange seller and actress from Covent Garden, she was a most unsuitable mistress for the king. However, Charles was entranced by her looks and wit. He took Nell Gwyn from the streets of Covent Garden to his royal palace, and had two children with her.

The English people loved 'pretty, witty Nelly'. On one occasion, Charles's coach was attacked by an angry mob, who accused Nell of being a 'Catholic whore'. She leaned out of the window and reassured them, 'I am the *Protestant* whore'. When Charles II died, he asked on his deathbed 'Let not poor Nelly starve'. She was provided with an annual pension of £1500 for the rest of her life.

Check your understanding

1. How did life for normal English people change during the Restoration?
2. What other movements inspired England's scientific revolution during the 17th century?
3. What was Sir Isaac Newton's theory of gravity able to explain?
4. How was the response to the Great Plague different from the response to the Black Death in 1348?
5. Why was Nell Gwyn seen as an unsuitable mistress for the king?

Unit 5: Commonwealth and Restoration
The Great Fire of London

The summer of 1666 was long and hot. By the time September came, London's medieval houses, which were made out of wood and straw, were tinder-box dry.

The king's baker, Thomas Farynor, lived not far from London Bridge on Pudding Lane. On 2 September, he left his ovens on overnight cooking biscuits for the Royal Navy, and awoke to the smell of burning. Thomas escaped by jumping out of his window, but his bakery was soon engulfed in flames.

Thanks to a warm wind, the fire quickly spread to the riverside. Here, the warehouses of the London docks were full of flammable goods such as tallow, oil, timber and coal. Once these caught light, the fire was unstoppable. Soon, the flames were raging through London so quickly that people saw flying pigeons burned in the air.

Contemporary painting of the Great Fire, looking west across the Thames. St Paul's Cathedral can be seen engulfed in flames in the distance.

Stopping the fire

It was left to the Mayor of London, Sir Thomas Bloodworth, to work out how to stop the fire. During the 17th century, there were no firemen or fire engines, and only the most basic water pumps and hoses. Teams of people lined up alongside the Thames passing leather buckets of water towards the flames. Even Charles II and his brother James took part in the fight. However, it made little difference and for three days, London was ablaze. The fire was so bright that at night an orange glow could be seen on the horizon 50 miles away in Oxford.

The only solution to the fire was to create **'firebreaks'**. To do this, rows of houses had to be pulled down with fire hooks or blown up with gunpowder, to create a barrier over which the fire could not pass. Many Londoners objected to having their houses or businesses, which had so far survived the flames, deliberately destroyed. However, the King overruled their objections, and the fire finally stopped on 7 September.

In all, the Great Fire claimed 13 200 houses, along with 87 churches, 44 merchant guildhalls, and all of the commercial buildings of the City of London. The medieval heart of England's capital was completely destroyed.

Rebuilding London

100 000 Londoners were left homeless by the fire and forced to live in tents outside the city. There was much speculation about how the fire began. Many rumours spread about Catholic plotters. A mad French watchmaker named Robert Hubert even admitted to starting the fire on the orders of the Pope, and was executed.

After the fire, Charles II set about the task of rebuilding London. To prevent another fire, it was firmly stated that buildings should only be constructed from brick or stone. The most talented architect of the day, Sir Christopher Wren, was tasked with designing a gleaming new London with wide streets, sewers and stone houses. At the centre of this new city was Wren's masterpiece: **St Paul's Cathedral**.

St Paul's Cathedral, London, England

Pepys' diary

Much can be learnt about life during the Restoration from a government official who worked in the Royal Navy named Samuel Pepys, who kept a wonderfully detailed diary from 1660 to 1669. It provides us with a unique insight into 17th century life.

Pepys was a sociable fellow, with connections at the royal court. He chatted to King Charles II on board the *Royal Charles*, the ship that brought him from Holland to England in 1660, and recorded: "…it made me weep to hear the stories he told of his difficulties he passed through".

Pepys was in London during the Great Fire, and took care to bury his most prized possession in his garden: a block of Parmesan cheese. On 3 September, he described seeing the crowds of people flee the city: "Lord! to see how the streets and the highways are crowded with people running and riding, and getting of carts at any rate to fetch away things. I am eased at my heart to have my treasure so well secured." The next day he wrote, "Only now and then walking into the garden, and saw how horridly the sky looks, all on a fire in the night." Pepys recorded how, as he walked towards central London during the fire, the road felt hot beneath his feet.

Samuel Pepys

Fact

Because the Great Fire took place in 1666, and the Great Plague attacked London the previous year, many believed that the four horsemen of the apocalypse were being sent to England as it was the 'year of the devil'.

Check your understanding

1. Why was London particularly vulnerable to fire at the end of the summer of 1666?

2. How did firebreaks stop the spread of the Great Fire?

3. What group of people were initially blamed for starting the Great Fire of London?

4. What rules did Christopher Wren have to follow when charged with rebuilding London after the fire?

5. Why is Samuel Pepys such an important guide for historians into life in 17th century England?

Unit 5: Commonwealth and Restoration
The Glorious Revolution

Despite having many children, Charles II died with no legitimate heir. This meant that his Catholic brother James II became king in 1685.

Many in England had feared this event. In 1679, a group in Parliament even tried to pass a bill excluding James II from the throne, but it was defeated in the House of Lords. A keen believer in the divine right of kings, James II dismissed Parliament the year that he was crowned.

Opponents to James II devised a new plan. The Duke of Monmouth was an **illegitimate** son of Charles II, and he was also a respected military commander and staunch Protestant. In 1685, Monmouth declared himself king and began a rebellion against James II in the West Country. James II's army easily defeated Monmouth's unimpressive force of 3000 men, and his response was savage.

James II, England's last Catholic monarch

Monmouth pleaded for forgiveness and promised to convert to Catholicism, but he was executed. Of his supporters, 850 were sent to the West Indies to work as slaves, and 480 were executed. Their severed heads were pickled in jars of vinegar and sent around England, as a warning to those who would still consider rebelling against their new king.

James II's reign

James II then began suspending the Test Acts, allowing Catholics back into public office. Protestant clergymen who criticised James II were tried for treason. James and his second wife, an Italian Catholic called Mary of Modena, had been married for 15 years and were childless. But then in June 1688, Mary gave birth to a son, also called James. This startling news all but guaranteed a Catholic future for the English throne.

The Duke of Monmouth

England's leading Protestants knew they had to act. Previously, James II had been married to an Englishwoman, Anne Hyde. With her, he had had two daughters, and the eldest – Mary – was third in line to the throne. She was married to the Dutch prince William of Orange, who also happened to be a grandson of Charles I, and Mary's first cousin. William and Mary were both staunch Protestants. On 30 June 1688, a group of seven leading English politicians wrote to William of Orange imploring him to invade England, and rid them of their Catholic king.

The Glorious Revolution

In the autumn of 1688, William of Orange began assembling an enormous invasion force of 463 ships and 40 000 troops in Holland. On 5 November they landed off the coast of Devon.

James II was outraged: his own daughter and son-in-law had invaded England to seize his crown. But James doubted whether he could rely on the support of the English people, so he decided not to fight. Increasingly

> ### Fact
> Many Protestants refused to believe that James II's son with Mary of Modena was real. A rumour spread that he was a miller's son, smuggled into the royal bed in a long-handled warming pan.

distraught, James II suffered a mental breakdown, and on 11 December he fled the Palace of Whitehall for exile in France. As he sailed from his palace, he threw the **Great Seal** of England into the Thames. Six weeks later, on 13 February 1689, William and Mary were crowned joint King and Queen of England.

Some historians claim it was an invasion, others claim it was a liberation, but all agree the events of 1688 changed England forever. This event later became known as the **'Glorious Revolution'**. It was a 'Revolution' because the people of England had ejected a Catholic absolutist as king, and replaced him with a Protestant king who was willing to rule with Parliament. It was 'Glorious' because not a single drop of blood was shed in the process. To secure the support of Parliament, William and Mary signed an agreement in 1689 called **the Bill of Rights**. This was a landmark document in securing legal and political rights for the people of England. Like Magna Carta before it, the Bill of Rights constrained the power of the English monarch.

Contemporary painting of William III's invasion force leaving Holland for England on 19th October, 1688

James II did not give up his claim to the English throne, and launched a rebellion from Ireland. He was defeated at the Battle of the Boyne in 1690, and went into exile with his wife and son in France, and then Rome. After 40 years of absolutism, civil war, regicide, dictatorship, restoration, and invasion, Parliament finally had their rights established in law. An absolute monarch would never again rule England.

The Bill of Rights

Some clauses of the Bill of Rights included:

- No Catholic could sit on the English throne
- Members of Parliament should have freedom of speech within Parliament (a principle known as Parliamentary prerogative)
- No taxes could be imposed on the people without the agreement of Parliament
- The king should not have a standing army during peacetime without the agreement of Parliament
- The king could not create or suspend laws without the agreement of Parliament

Check your understanding

1. Once made king, how did James II try to rule as an 'absolute monarch'?

2. Who were William and Mary, and what was their claim to the throne?

3. Why is William and Mary's invasion known as the Glorious Revolution?

4. How did the Bill of Rights ensure the power of Parliament was established in law?

5. What became of James II following the Glorious Revolution?

Unit 5: Commonwealth and Restoration
Knowledge organiser

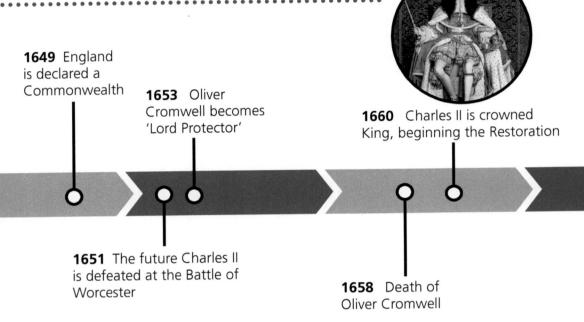

1649 England is declared a Commonwealth

1653 Oliver Cromwell becomes 'Lord Protector'

1660 Charles II is crowned King, beginning the Restoration

1651 The future Charles II is defeated at the Battle of Worcester

1658 Death of Oliver Cromwell

Key vocabulary

Commonwealth The period when England ceased to be a monarchy, and was at first ruled by Parliament

Declaration of Breda A series of promises made by Charles II prior to his restoration as king

Exile Being forced to live outside your native country, typically for political reasons

Firebreaks A manmade gap in combustible material used to prevent the further spread of fire

Glorious Revolution The peaceful rejection of James II as king, and replacement by William and Mary

Godly Providence A belief that events are governed by the direct intervention of God in the world

Great Seal A seal used to show the monarch's approval of important state documents

Illegitimate Not recognised as lawful, once used to describe someone born of unmarried parents

Lord Protector The title given to Oliver Cromwell as head of the English state and the Church of England

Merry Monarch Nickname given to Charles II due to his wit, lack of seriousness, and fun-loving lifestyle

Miasma The theory that disease is caused by the spreading smell of a poisonous cloud of 'bad air'

Military Dictatorship A form of government where the military hold sole power over the state

Plague The most common variant is Bubonic plague, named after the swellings on victims' bodies

Rational thought The idea that reasoning, not superstition, should be the source of human knowledge

Regicide The deliberate killing of a monarch, or the person responsible for doing so

Restoration The return of the monarchy to England with Charles II's coronation in 1660

Royal Society A group founded in 1660 for the advancement of scientific knowledge

Rump Parliament The remaining members of the Parliament after it was purged before Charles I's trial

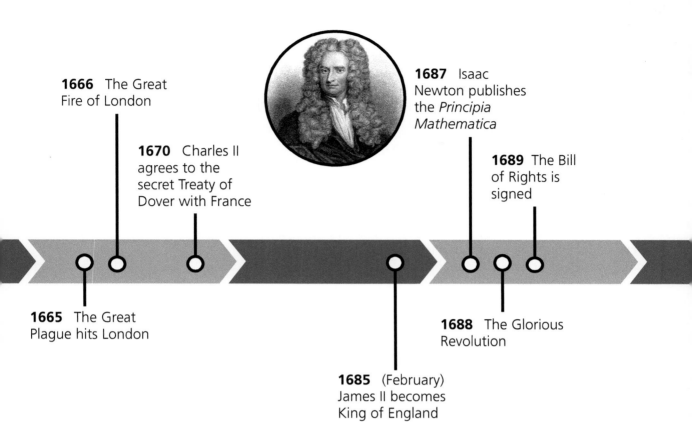

1666 The Great Fire of London

1670 Charles II agrees to the secret Treaty of Dover with France

1687 Isaac Newton publishes the *Principia Mathematica*

1689 The Bill of Rights is signed

1665 The Great Plague hits London

1688 The Glorious Revolution

1685 (February) James II becomes King of England

Key people

Charles II The King of England following the Restoration

Duke of Monmouth Illegitimate son of Charles II who led a rebellion against James II and was executed

James II The brother of Charles II, who was forced to abdicate after three years of absolutist rule

Nell Gwyn Charles II's mistress rose from being an actress to being a member of the royal court

Oliver Cromwell A Parliamentary cavalry general, who became Lord Protector of England

Samuel Pepys Official in the Royal Navy during the reign of Charles II, who kept a famous diary

Sir Christopher Wren Architect who rebuilt St Paul's Cathedral following the Great Fire of London

Sir Isaac Newton A great scientist, often said to be the founder of modern physics

William and Mary Joint monarchs from 1688: one a Dutch prince, the other a daughter of James II

Key vocabulary

Scientific Revolution The emergence of modern scientific methods during the 17th and 18th centuries

St Paul's Cathedral Historic London Cathedral, destroyed during and rebuilt after the Great Fire

Superstition The belief in supernatural powers, in place of rational explanation

Test Act A law requiring all those who held public office to be Protestants

The Bill of Rights A document establishing Parliament's rights and limitations to the Monarch's power

Treaty of Dover A secret treaty in which Charles II promised Louis XIV he would convert to Catholicism

Unit 6: Georgian Britain
Creation of Great Britain

William and Mary, who became joint king and queen following the Glorious Revolution, were succeeded by Mary's sister Anne in 1702. Queen Anne was England's last Stuart monarch.

Anne's life was cursed with bad luck. She suffered from a horrible illness called **gout**, and not one of her 18 children survived long enough to succeed her. Anne had seven miscarriages, six stillbirths, and five children who died young. Despite all of these troubles, she was a wise and important queen, and it was during her reign that the nation of **Great Britain** was created.

Statue of Queen Anne, beside St Paul's Cathedral, London, England

The creation of Great Britain

Parliament was very worried about Queen Anne's lack of children. Her Catholic half-brother James Stuart, son of James II, had been brought up in France and believed that he should be king of England. He had the support of the powerful kings of France and Spain.

To avoid another civil war, the English Parliament had passed the **Act of Settlement** in 1701, declaring that when Anne died, the crown would pass to her nearest Protestant relative. Most people in England were happy with the settlement, but the Scottish people were not. Since 1603 the same monarch had ruled Scotland and England, but they had remained two separate countries, with two separate parliaments.

The Scots were furious that they were not consulted about who would succeed Queen Anne. Many in Scotland liked the idea of being ruled by James Stuart. The Stuart family was originally from Scotland, and a number of powerful Scottish families were still Catholics. So, in 1703 the Scottish Parliament declared that when Queen Anne died, they would choose their own monarch. This would have broken the 100-year union between the English and Scottish crowns.

The English were very worried about this development. They proposed to Scotland that their two countries should become one, sharing one monarch, with one Parliament based in Westminster. At first the Scots disliked this idea: the English writer Daniel Defoe travelled to Scotland and reported: "for every Scot in favour there is 99 against".

However, the Scottish people had recently invested £500 000 (half the nation's available capital) in an adventurous plan to establish a Scottish colony in Central America, known as the **Darien Scheme**. It was a terrible failure, and very nearly bankrupted the country. Therefore, the English

Parliament was able to win round the Scottish leaders with some very generous bribes. The Scottish Parliament agreed to vote itself into non-existence. On 1 May 1707, the **Act of Union** was passed. The Scottish poet Robert Burns later wrote of the Act, "We're bought and sold for English gold, such a parcel of rogues in a nation!"

The first article of the Act of Union declared "That the two Kingdoms of England and Scotland shall upon the first day of May… be united into one Kingdom by the name of Great Britain." The Act also described the flag that this new country would use, combining the diagonal white cross of St Andrew, and the red cross of St George. This new national flag was nicknamed the **'Union Jack'**.

The Hanoverian succession

Queen Anne had been ill for many years, and died in 1714. Her doctor wrote, "I believe sleep was never more welcome to a weary traveller than death was to her". So, Parliament set about searching Europe for Anne's closest surviving Protestant relative to be her successor. The answer was found in the shape of Georg Ludwig, the 54-year-old ruler of a small German state called Hanover. He just happened to be the great-grandson of James I.

Georg Ludwig arrived in London on 18 September with a procession of 260 horse-drawn carriages, and was crowned George I of Great Britain a month later. Britain now had a new royal family, known as the **Hanoverians**.

For many people, it was a strange sight. There were 57 Catholic descendents of the Stuarts across Europe with a better claim to the English throne than George I. Before being plucked from obscurity to become King, George I had only visited England once in his life. He spoke no English and took very little interest in the country, preferring to spend his time playing cards, visiting Germany, and entertaining his two mistresses. They were nicknamed the elephant and the maypole because one was very fat, and the other was very thin.

> **Fact**
>
> George I was famous for his temper. While he was Elector of Hanover, he had found out his wife was unfaithful, so he locked her in a tower for the rest of her life.

Painting of George I, who went from ruling a small German state to becoming King of Great Britain in 1714

Check your understanding

1. Why were many people in Scotland opposed to the Act of Settlement?
2. Why did the English Parliament propose in 1703 that England and Scotland become one country?
3. How did the English Parliament manage to win round the Scots into supporting the Act of Union?
4. Why did George I become king in 1714 when 57 people across Europe had a better claim to the throne?
5. Where had George I ruled before he was crowned King of Great Britain?

Unit 6: Georgian Britain
Parliamentary government

Although George I was king, he knew almost nothing about how to rule Britain. For this reason he relied on his **ministers**, normally Members of Parliament, to make decisions on his behalf.

After an unhappy century of absolutist monarchs causing disagreements and wars, this new situation suited Parliament very nicely. From now on, the monarch reigned but ministers ruled.

Britain's first Prime Minister, Sir Robert Walpole

The first Prime Minister

Robert Walpole was a wealthy farmer from Norfolk and a Member of Parliament. He weighed 20 stone, loved drinking and eating, and had ambitions to become the most powerful politician in Britain. Walpole's political career took off after an economic crash called **the South Sea Bubble** (see box). Walpole was made Paymaster General and successfully restored Britain's economy, becoming George I's favourite minister as a result.

Walpole was not an honest man. He would bribe other politicians to get his way. As a young man he even spent six months imprisoned in the Tower of London for corruption! One of his favourite sayings was that "all men have their price". However, Walpole was a popular figure and good at his job.

In 1721, Walpole was given three of the key jobs in British politics: First Lord of the Treasury, Chancellor of the Exchequer and Leader of the **House of Commons**. This made him the most important minister in the King's Government, so people would refer to him as the **'prime' minister**. The king gave him a house in London

10 Downing Street, London, England

to live in, and selected number 10 on a new development near Parliament called 'Downing Street'. Walpole recommended that the house should forever remain the property of whoever held his position. To this day the Prime Minister of Great Britain lives at number **10 Downing Street**.

Parliamentary government

In 1727 King George I died, and his son George II became king. George II spoke a bit more English, but with a heavy German accent. He thought Walpole had become too powerful as Prime Minister, and tried to replace him. However, Walpole promised George II that, if he was kept as Prime Minister, he would increase the king's allowance. Since the Glorious Revolution, Parliament controlled the monarch's annual allowance – something known as the 'power of the purse'. So, George II decided to let Walpole keep his job.

> **Fact**
>
> In 1755 George II visited Hanover and considered not returning to Britain because he was so angry at the growing power of Parliament. He complained, "Ministers are the kings in this country, I am nothing there."

As Prime Minister, Walpole had two ambitions: to stay out of any foreign wars, and to keep taxes low. He succeeded, and Britain grew wealthy as her foreign trade flourished. Walpole once boasted to Queen Caroline, the wife of George II, "Madam, there are 50 000 men slain this year in Europe, and not one Englishman".

During the 20 years that Walpole was in power, he established **'parliamentary government'** in Great Britain. In theory the king could choose his government ministers, but in reality he could only choose those with the support of the most powerful party in Parliament. Parliament was, as it still is today, split into two 'Houses': the Commons and the Lords. Seats in the House of Commons went to Members of Parliament elected by the British public, though only a small minority of wealthy men had the vote. Most seats in the **House of Lords** passed down through generations of noble families along with hereditary titles, which were – in order of importance – Duke, Marquess, Earl, Viscount, and Baron.

Painting of the Prime Minister addressing the House of Commons, from the end of the eighteenth century

By this time, two rival political parties had developed in Parliament, each with different ideas about how England should be governed. One party wanted to limit the power of the king and allow greater tolerance for religious groups. They were nicknamed **'Whigs'**—an old Scottish insult for Presbyterian rebels. The other group wanted to protect the power of the king and the Church of England. They were nicknamed **'Tories'**—an old Irish word for a Catholic outlaw.

The South Sea Bubble

The South Sea Bubble was one of the greatest economic disasters in British history. Exclusive rights to trade with Spanish colonies in South America were granted to the South Sea Company, and company **shares** became highly sought after. Over the spring of 1720, its share price increased by ten times, but then the bubble burst and the share price came crashing down.

Thousands of normal citizens who had invested in the company were made bankrupt overnight, company directors fled the country, and a spate of suicides took place. One government minister, Lord Stanhope, even died of a stroke during an angry debate in Parliament.

Check your understanding:

1. How did Robert Walpole become George I's favourite minister?
2. How was the role of Prime Minster established during Walpole's time in power?
3. How did the system of parliamentary government, established by Walpole, function?
4. Why did George II consider not returning from Hanover when he visited in 1755?
5. What caused the South Sea Bubble to take place?

Unit 6: Georgian Britain
Jacobite uprisings

Most people in Britain were by now happy with their new German kings, but a small group retained a passionate belief that the Stuart royal family should still be governing Britain.

These people called themselves **'Jacobites'**, a name taken from the Latin word for 'James'. They formed secret societies across England and Scotland, and plotted to overthrow the Hanoverian kings. In 1715, a small Jacobite rebellion failed to place James II's son, James Stuart, on the throne. But they kept on plotting – waiting for the right moment to act.

Bonnie Prince Charlie

By 1745 the British army was busy fighting the French in Europe, so the Jacobites spotted a chance. Support for the Stuart claim to the throne was strongest in the mountains and moors of the Scottish **Highlands**. Ancient **'clans'** ruled this part of Scotland, and each clan was led by a 'chief'. The clansmen were mostly poor Catholic farmers, but they were also fierce warriors who believed the 1707 Act of Union had robbed Scotland of its independence.

Painting of Bonnie Prince Charlie with two clan chiefs, completed in 1892

The Jacobites found a new hope in James Stuart's eldest son, Charles Edward Stuart, who was a charismatic and brave soldier. He was also very good looking, so his Highland supporters named him 'Bonnie Prince Charlie' – 'Bonnie' meaning good-looking in Scotland. Prince Charlie landed in Scotland in July 1745, and the Highland clans rushed to welcome him. They raised enough men to take Edinburgh, the capital city of Scotland, and routed the small British army in Scotland at the Battle of Prestonpans.

The Highlanders wore Scottish **tartan** and caps with white cockades, and armed themselves with traditional Scottish swords called **claymores**. With these soldiers, Prince Charlie won a series of victories in Scotland, and by November his 6000 men were marching south towards London. With most of his army fighting in France, King George II was terrified. He even loaded a boat on the Thames with treasure so that he could make an easy escape if Prince Charlie's army arrived in London.

Prince Charlie expected that England's Jacobites, who for years had held underground meetings and identified each other through secret symbols, would rush to his support when he invaded England. When the moment came, however, most were not brave enough to risk their lives. Prince Charlie marched as far south as Derby, but his soldiers grew disheartened about the lack of support from the English people. On 5 December 1745, the Jacobite army began its retreat back to the Scottish Highlands.

The Battle of Culloden

By now, George II had raised an army led by his son the Duke of Cumberland and put a price of £30 000 on Prince Charlie's head.

Cumberland's red-coated soldiers shadowed the retreating Jacobites to the Highlands of Scotland, where they met for a final battle at Culloden Moor in April 1746. Cumberland defeated the Jacobite army in less than an hour, tearing them apart with his cannons and cavalry.

Bonnie Prince Charlie escaped from the battlefield, and for weeks he hid in the moors of Scotland. According to legend, he was found by a young woman named Flora MacDonald who planned his escape. MacDonald disguised Prince Charlie as her Irish maid, and he took a boat to the Isle of Skye, and from there he escaped to France.

Prince Charlie lived the rest of his life in exile in Italy. The Stuart cause was dead, and the Hanoverians were safely established as Britain's royal family. Culloden remains the last ever battle to be fought on British soil.

> **Fact**
>
> Prince Charlie died in Rome on 31 January 1788 the anniversary of his great-great-grandfather Charles I's execution in 1649.

Contemporary painting of the Battle of Culloden

Suppression of the Highlands

The British Government wanted to make sure that no Jacobite rising could ever happen again. Cumberland hunted down and killed all of the remaining Jacobite soldiers with such savagery that he became known as 'the Butcher'. The British Government did not stop there. They made it illegal for Highlanders to wear their traditional dress of tartan and kilts, or to own weapons. The right of the chiefs to rule their own clans was abolished, and many Highland farmers were forced to move to the Scottish lowlands, or emigrate to America.

A large barracks named **Fort George** was built outside Inverness so that the British army could keep a watchful eye on their troublesome fellow countrymen north of the border. From now on, the Scottish Highlands were firmly under the control of the British Government.

Memorial to the Jacobites, at Glenfinnan, Highlands, Scotland

Check your understanding:
1. Why did Jacobites oppose the Hanoverian kings?
2. Why did many of Scotland's highland clans support Bonnie Prince Charlie?
3. Why did Bonnie Prince Charlie's army retreat back to Scotland in December 1745?
4. What happened at the Battle of Culloden?
5. How did the British government ensure that no Jacobite rising could ever happen again in Scotland?

Unit 6: Georgian Britain
Georgian aristocracy

Parliamentary government in Georgian Britain may have weakened the power of the monarch, but power did not move to the people.

Instead, power became increasingly concentrated in the hands of Britain's nobility, leading many historians to call the 18th century the 'Age of **Aristocracy'**. There were 173 **peers** in the House of Lords in 1700, and the great majority of government ministers came from this closed circle of titled landowners. England's first 10 Prime Ministers included three dukes, one marquess, two earls, and two who became earls during their lifetime.

Powerful families such as the Temples dominated English politics: Earl Temple and all four of his brothers served as members of Parliament, with one – George Grenville – becoming Prime Minister. Meanwhile, their sister Hester married William Pitt, who later became Prime Minister and the Earl of Chatham, and whose son, Pitt the Younger, also served as Prime Minister.

When a peer had no sons to inherit his title, it would become extinct, so the king regularly had to create new peerages. However, breaking into this class from a humble background was almost impossible: of the 229 peerages created between 1700 and 1800, only 23 had no previous connection with the aristocracy. Though they sat in the House of Lords, the aristocracy still held influence over elections to the House of Commons. MPs in the Commons were often related by birth or marriage to the aristocracy, and in 1715, 224 of the 558 members of the House of Commons were the sons of MPs.

The Georgian aristocracy grew increasingly wealthy during this period, often acquiring more land from the gentry, whose wealth was in decline. Aristocratic stately homes, such as Castle Howard and Blenheim Palace, remain some of the most extravagant buildings in Britain. Wentworth Woodhouse in Yorkshire, home to the 2nd Marquess of Rockingham (who became Prime Minister in 1765), is Britain's largest stately home, with over 300 rooms.

Painting of Mr and Mrs Andrews, a wealthy couple from the landed gentry, completed in 1750

Fact

A powerful Whig politician, Charles James Fox, inherited one of the largest fortunes in Georgian England, but he loved to gamble. Fox went bankrupt twice, had his furniture confiscated by bailiffs, and by the time of his death had gambled away £200 000 – perhaps £18 million in today's money.

Wentworth Castle in Yorkshire, England

Leisure and entertainment

The Georgian aristocracy and gentry certainly knew how to enjoy themselves. Horseracing, card games, hunting, theatre, the opera, and – most notably – gambling were all popular amongst the Georgian elite. They drank and gambled at exclusive London clubs such as Brooks' and White's, and visited fashionable holiday towns such as Brighton and Bath, which are still famous for their fine Georgian architecture.

For half of the year, from January to June, Parliament was in session, so the aristocracy decamped from their country estates to their smart London townhouses. Known as the **'season'**, this period was accompanied by a whirl of glamorous parties and events. A collection of fields to the west of London where the May Fair took place each year, had recently been developed by its owner Sir Thomas Grosvenor into townhouses. This new development became known as Mayfair, and at its centre lay Grosvenor Square, the most fashionable address in London.

Scene from 'Marriage à la mode', a series of paintings by William Hogarth satirising aristocratic life

Having the right tastes in fashion and art was very important to the Georgian aristocracy, and they often acted as patrons to young writers and artists. For the sons of Britain's aristocracy, the best way to finish their education was to undertake a **'Grand Tour'** of Europe. Lasting around two years, young aristocratic men on a Grand Tour learned about the culture and history of Europe – in particular Italy.

While travelling, these young aristocrats bought artefacts from Ancient Rome, fashionable European clothes, and paintings by celebrated artists, such as the Venetian painter Canaletto. However, many young aristocrats set free in Europe took a different path, spending their money on drinking, gambling and womanising instead.

Samuel Johnson

The son of a poor bookseller from Lichfield, Samuel Johnson worked his way to the University of Oxford and onwards to becoming one of the greatest writers in the English language. He was famously ugly, and had lots of nervous tics. However, because he was so witty and intelligent, his company was highly sought after by the Georgian aristocracy, in particular his lifelong friend and biographer James Boswell.

After 10 years of work, Johnson published one of the first English language dictionaries in 1755. It contained the definitions for 40 000 words. These included some amusing entries. Johnson defined 'dull' as "Not exhilarating; not delightful; as, to make dictionaries is dull work".

Check your understanding

1. How many aristocratic peers were there in England at the beginning of the 18th century?
2. How did the aristocracy still have power over the House of Commons?
3. Why did the aristocracy spend half of the year in London, and half of the year in their stately homes?
4. What would young aristocrats do while they undertook the Grand Tour?
5. What achievement is Samuel Johnson best remembered for?

Unit 6: Georgian Britain
Poverty, violence and crime

While the power and wealth of Georgian Britain flowed to the aristocracy, many in Britain's towns and cities lived lives of poverty, violence and crime.

Some of the worst poverty was to be found in London, where people moved to find work, but sudden joblessness could make them destitute. The poorest families lived in single, unfurnished rooms, with no running water or sanitation.

For those who could not afford a room, vagrancy was the only alternative. It was not uncommon to find dead bodies on the streets of major cities, particularly on cold winter mornings. In 1753, a writer called Henry Fielding described the streets of London as "oppressed with hunger, cold, nakedness and filth… There is not a street that does not swarm all day with beggars, and all night with thieves".

Many of the poor drowned their sorrows with a newly popular drink called gin. Cheap and strong, it was said that in 1730s London there was a shop selling gin for every 11 people. George II's Vice-Chamberlain observed "the whole town of London swarmed with drunken people from morning till night." Gin was blamed for a host of social problems, from violence and robberies to murders, irreligion and child mortality. This can be seen in the vivid print *Gin Lane*, created by William Hogarth in 1751 (see box).

William Hogarth's print 'Gin Lane', showing the social consequences of gin addiction amongst the Georgian poor

Whenever Parliament tried to control the trade of gin with licensing acts, the people of London would riot. In 1736, Parliament introduced an annual £50 licence which shopkeepers had to buy in order to sell gin. In response, angry crowds spread through London chanting "No gin, no king!". The 1751 Gin Act succeeded in placing a tax on the drink, and began a decline in gin's popularity.

Law and order

Georgian Britain could be a strikingly violent place. The right to bear arms was enshrined in the 1689 Bill of Rights, so that the Protestant population could arm themselves against the Catholic threat. Members of the aristocracy commonly carried swords, and pistols were easy to purchase. As the century went on, these weapons were increasingly used for violent crime.

There was no organised police force in Georgian Britain. While smaller towns and villages were able to govern themselves, in the growing towns and cities violent crime became a severe problem. Criminals would break

> **Fact**
>
> Even dead bodies would be stolen in Georgian England. 'Body snatchers' robbed newly dug graves, and sold the corpses to trainee doctors and anatomists who used them for dissections.

into houses, rob passers-by on the streets, and steal cargo from ships. Crime waves often followed the end of foreign wars, when industry would slump due to the army no longer needing supplies, and soldiers would return home unable to find jobs.

For criminals facing trial, Georgian prisons were frequently likened to hell on earth. Many prisons were run as private, profit-making organisations, so prisoners were kept in horrific conditions to keep costs low. Human waste lined the floors of overcrowded and windowless cells, which were freezing cold in the winter and unbearably hot in the summer. Newgate was the most notorious of all London's prisons. During the 18th century, Newgate suffered repeated outbreaks of typhus, a fatal disease spread by lice. Prisoners would often escape by breaking through the floor of their cells and exiting through the sewer.

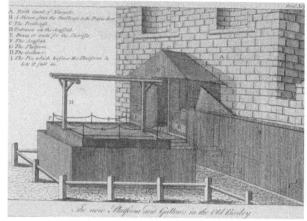

Platform and gallows at Newgate Prison, Old Bailey, City of London, 1783

Highwaymen

The 18th century saw an increase in **highwaymen:** armed robbers on horseback who attacked people travelling in **stagecoaches** along dark, empty roads. The use of cheques only became common during the second half of the century, so people often had to carry large sums of money in person. Travellers came to dread the sound of galloping hooves and pistol shots, followed by the infamous cry "Stand and Deliver! Your money or your life!"

Grave and headstone of Dick Turpin

The most well known highwayman was Dick Turpin. Today he is remembered as a dashing hero, but in reality he was a convicted murderer who terrorised the roads of Essex until he was hanged at York in 1739.

William Hogarth

Perhaps the greatest artist of Georgian Britain was William Hogarth. His father was an impoverished Latin teacher, and Hogarth spent his childhood drawing caricatures of London street life. He came to specialise in **satirical** cartoons, often criticising the moral failings of Georgian society, such as its addiction to gin.

Hogarth's works liked to tell a story. His series of paintings known as *A Rake's Progress* follows the son of a wealthy merchant who wastes all of his money on fine clothes, women and gambling, before becoming bankrupt and being sent to a mental asylum.

Check your understanding

1. In cities such as London, what sort of conditions did the poorest in society have to live in?
2. What happened when Parliament tried to control the sale of gin during the 18th century?
3. Why was crime particularly serious during the Georgian period following the end of foreign wars?
4. Why did 18th century highwaymen target people who were travelling?
5. What were conditions like in 18th century prisons?

Unit 6: Georgian Britain
Knowledge organiser

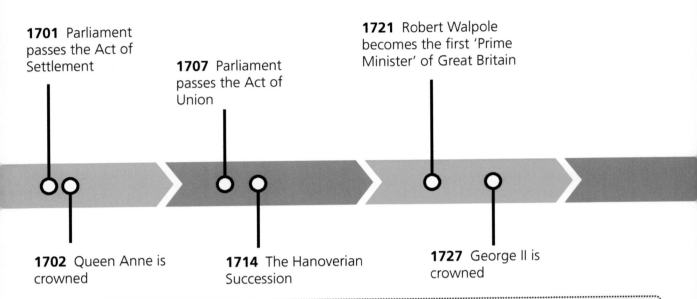

1701 Parliament passes the Act of Settlement

1707 Parliament passes the Act of Union

1721 Robert Walpole becomes the first 'Prime Minister' of Great Britain

1702 Queen Anne is crowned

1714 The Hanoverian Succession

1727 George II is crowned

Key vocabulary

10 Downing Street Traditional home of the English Prime Minister since the reign of George I

Act of Settlement A law passed in 1701 ensuring that a Protestant would succeed Queen Anne

Act of Union A law which united England and Scotland in 1707, and created Great Britain

Aristocracy The government of a country by an elite class, often with hereditary titles

Clan Ancient family from the Highlands of Scotland

Claymore A traditional Scottish sword

Darien Scheme A failed attempt by the Scottish government to establish a Caribbean trading colony

Fort George A large British barracks built in the Scottish Highlands following Jacobite defeat

Gout An illness caused by heavy eating or drinking, which causes joints to become swollen

Grand Tour Journey taken by upper class young men to experience the art and culture of Europe

Great Britain A name given to the island comprising England, Wales and Scotland

Hanoverians A royal dynasty that ruled England from 1714 until 1837

Highlands A sparsely populated area of northern Scotland known for its mountainous landscape

Highwaymen Armed robbers on horseback who attacked people travelling in stagecoaches

House of Commons The 'lower house' in Parliament, where seats go to MPs elected by the people

House of Lords The 'upper house' in Parliament, where seats are inherited by members of the peerage

Jacobite Supporters of the Stuart claim to the throne, following the exile of James II

Minister A politician with a central role within the nation's government

Parliamentary government A political system where ministers must be chosen from the most powerful party in Parliament

Peer A member of the House of Lords who, for most of English history, were from the nobility

Prime Minister The most senior post in the British government, first held by Sir Robert Walpole

Satirical Using humour to criticise human failings, often in the context of politics

Season A six-month period when Parliament was in session and the aristocracy came to London

Share A portion of a company that can be bought, bringing with it a portion of the profits

1739
The highwayman Dick Turpin is hanged in York

1746 The Battle of Culloden

1751 Parliament pass the Gin Act

1745 Bonnie Prince Charlie leads a Jacobite uprising

1755 Samuel Johnson publishes his dictionary of the English language

Key vocabulary

Stagecoach A horse drawn carriage used for long distance travel

Suppression A dominant political power limiting the freedom and activity of a group of people

Tartan Traditional patterned cloth of Scotland, often used to make kilts

The South Sea Bubble An economic disaster caused by the sudden drop in share price of a colonial trading company

Tories A political party which originally formed to protect the power of the king

Union Jack Nickname for the national flag of Great Britain

Whigs A political party which originally formed to limit the power of the king

Key people

Bonnie Prince Charlie The last Stuart claimant to Britain's throne, and leader of a failed rebellion in 1745

Dick Turpin Legendary 18th century highwayman from Essex

Duke of Cumberland Son of George II, nicknamed 'the Butcher' for his suppression of the Highlands

George I The first Hanoverian King of England, previously a minor German prince

Queen Anne The last Stuart monarch, who created the union between England and Scotland

Robert Walpole A major Georgian statesman, generally seen as Britain's first Prime Minister

Samuel Johnson Famous Georgian writer, author of one of the first dictionaries of the English language

William Hogarth English satirical artist, his best known works are 'Gin Lane' and 'A Rake's Progress'.

Index

Acknowledgments

Thank you to all the friends, family, colleagues and former teachers who helped me to write this book. More people than I could mention have given up their time to read early drafts, fact check certain sections, and offer advice. I am hugely grateful for the generosity of you all.

Robert Peal

Every effort has been made to trace copyright holders and to obtain their permission for the use of copyright material. The publishers will gladly receive any information enabling them to rectify any error or omission at the first opportunity. The publishers would like to thank the following for permission to reproduce copyright material:

(t = top, b = bottom, c = centre, l = left, r = right)

Cover & p1 © Victoria and Albert Museum, London; p6 Heritage Image Partnership Ltd/Alamy; p7t GL Archive/Alamy; p7b Lebrecht Music and Arts Photo Library/Alamy; p8t FALKENSTEINFOTO/Alamy; p8b Ignatius Tan/Shutterstock; p9 imageBROKER/Alamy; p10t Mary Evans Picture Library/Alamy; p10c IanDagnall Computing/Alamy; p10b GL Archive/Alamy; p11 Ian Shaw/Alamy; p12t National Portrait Gallery, London, UK/Bridgeman Images; p12b Loop Images Ltd/Alamy; p13 His Grace The Duke of Norfolk, Arundel Castle/Bridgeman Images; p14 Antiques & Collectables/Alamy; p15 ACTIVE MUSEUM/Alamy; p15 Photology1971/Shutterstock; p18t Vatican Museums and Galleries, Vatican City/Bridgeman Images; p18b kavalenkava volha/Shutterstock; p19 Pinacoteca di Brera, Milan, Italy/Bridgeman Images; p20 Dja65/Shutterstock; p21t dinosmichail/Shutterstock; p21b Everett - Art/Shutterstock; p22t Nithid/Shutterstock; p22b North Wind Picture Archives/Alamy; p23 Classic Image/Alamy; p24t imageBROKER/Alamy; p24b Everett Historical/Shutterstock; p25 Michael Rosskothen/Shutterstock; p26t Anna Omelchenko/Shutterstock; p26b KasperKay/Shutterstock; p27 De Agostini Picture Library/Bridgeman Images; p28 Classic Image/Alamy; p30t Ian G Dagnall/Alamy; p30b Heritage Image Partnership Ltd/Alamy; p31t The Stapleton Collection/Bridgeman Images; p31b Granger Historical Picture Archve/Alamy; p32t World History Archive/Alamy; p32b Ian Dagnall/Alamy; p33r Steve Sant/Alamy; p33l Ian Dagnall/Alamy; p34t Stocksnapper/Shutterstock; p34b World History Archive/Alamy; p35t The Stapleton Collection/Bridgeman Images; p35b LOOK Die Bildagentur der Fotografen GmbH/Alamy; p36 World History Archive/Alamy; p37 National Geographic Creative/Alamy; p38t Hatfield House, Hertfordshire, UK/Bridgeman Images; p38b ACTIVE MUSEUM/Alamy; p39 Fotosearch/Stringer/Getty; p42 Lebrecht Music and Arts Photo Library/Alamy; p43t Mary Evans Picture Library/Alamy; p43b Private Collection/© Look and Learn/Bridgeman Images; p44t Private Collection/Bridgeman Images; p44b Palazzo Pitti, Florence, Italy/Bridgeman Images; p45 AlTimewatch Images/Alamy amy; p46 Ashmolean Museum, University of Oxford, UK/Bridgeman Images; p47 Houses of Parliament, Westminster, London, UK/Bridgeman Images; p48 Petworth House, West Sussex, UK/National Trust Photographic Library/Derrick E. Witty/Bridgeman Images; p49 © Look and Learn/Bridgeman Images; p50 Robert B. Miller/Shutterstock.com; p51t Private Collection/Bridgeman Images; p51b Ashmolean Museum, University of Oxford, UK/Bridgeman Images; p54 AlamGL Archive/Alamy; p55t Heritage Image Partnership Ltd/Alamy; p55b Stocktrek Images; Inc./Alamy; p56t AlamNiday Picture Library/Alamy; p56b Royal Collection Trust © Her Majesty Queen Elizabeth II, 2016/Bridgeman Images; p57 Granger Historical Picture Archve/Alamy; p58t World History Archive/Alamy; p58b Ala19th era/Alamy; p59t Granger Historical Picture Archve/Alamy; p59b GL Archive/Alamy; p60 GL Archive/Alamy; p61t TTstudio/Shutterstock; p61b GL Archive/Alamy; p62t World History Archive/Alamy; p62b Granger Historical Picture Archve/Alamy; p63 Royal Collection Trust © Her Majesty Queen Elizabeth II, 2016/Bridgeman Images; p66 David Jackson/Alamy; p67 GL Archive/Alamy; p68t Ian Dagnall/Alamy; p68b pcruciatti/Shutterstock.com; p69 Everett - Art/Shutterstock; p70 GL Archive/Alamy; p71t GL Archive/Alamy; p71b StevanZZ/Shutterstock; p72t The Artchives/Alamy; p72b Alastair Wallace/Shutterstock; p73t World History Archive/Alamy; p73b Peter Horree/Alamy; p74 Lebrecht Music and Arts Photo Library/Alamy; p75t Heritage Image Partnership Ltd/Alamy; p75b Holmes Garden Photos/Alamy